GHOSTLY
ADVENTURES

**CHILLING TRUE STORIES
FROM AMERICA'S
HAUNTED HOT SPOTS**

Christopher Balzano

Avon, Massachusetts

Copyright © 2008 by F+W Publications, Inc.
All rights reserved.
This book, or parts thereof, may not be reproduced in any
form without permission from the publisher; exceptions are
made for brief excerpts used in published reviews.

Published by
Adams Media, an F+W Publications Company
57 Littlefield Street, Avon, MA 02322. U.S.A.
www.adamsmedia.com

Contains material adopted and abridged from *The Everything® Ghost
Book* by Jason Rich, Copyright © 2001 by F+W Publications, Inc.

ISBN-10: 1-59869-679-3
ISBN-13: 978-1-59869-679-0

Printed in Canada.

J I H G F E D C B

Library of Congress Cataloging-in-Publication Data
is available from the publisher.

This publication is designed to provide accurate and authoritative
information with regard to the subject matter covered. It is sold with
the understanding that the publisher is not engaged in rendering legal,
accounting, or other professional advice. If legal advice or other expert
assistance is required, the services of a competent professional person
should be sought.
—From a *Declaration of Principles* jointly adopted by a Committee of the
American Bar Association and a Committee of Publishers and Associations

Many of the designations used by manufacturers and sellers to distin-
guish their product are claimed as trademarks. Where those designations
appear in this book and Adams Media was aware of a trademark claim,
the designations have been printed with initial capital letters.

Map copyright © iStock

*This book is available at quantity discounts for bulk purchases.
For information, please call 1-800-289-0963.*

CONTENTS

Contents

INTRODUCTION

What makes someone an expert on the paranormal? It's really the same thing that makes anyone an authority on anything; the only trouble is that paranormal experts specialize in something that hasn't been proven. A doctor knows, with some certainty, how a treatment will help someone, and an architect knows a foundation built the right way will support the weight of a certain number of floors. A paranormal investigator, an authority on things that go bump in the night, can't offer those kinds of guarantees. So an expert, the man to talk to about ghosts, is someone versed in the theories.

And the theories are out there. Although I have investigated the paranormal for more than fourteen years, I have maintained my Web site for only seven. When I first published it, I always referred to myself in the plural, although it was only me, in front of my computer, putting the pieces together. When I investigated a haunting, I looked to different people I trusted or who had certain skills. This has allowed me to work with many of the groups in New England and drift from one approach to another. The only thing I can say about this is that it has shown me there are no authorities. There are many groups out there doing good work, and no one comes from the same place on what a ghost is or how to make contact. But that is liberating.

A paranormal investigator, at his best, is open-minded. Show me what you do. Explain to me why you think it works. Does it make sense? Get enough ideas, and find the reasons behind them, and you too can become an expert. When I get a call about a haunting, and I get calls or e-mails every day, my mind runs through what I have experienced. But more importantly, I think of who might be the best person I know to tap for more information. Knowledge makes the expert, and knowing where to turn is the best way to gain that knowledge.

Think of reading this book as having a conversation with me about ghosts. I hope there is enough information here to give you some idea of what is out there. There is a bit of everything, but this book is far from all-inclusive. A sixth grader from Indiana recently e-mailed me and asked me how to get started in ghost hunting. He wanted to know how to do what I do. I told him not to buy one piece of equipment. Instead I suggested he hit the library and read all the information out there.

Read this book with an inquisitive mind. Question what I say, and challenge me on the point of view I offer you. This book is a resource, but hopefully it provides you with the tools to find the answers yourself.

Introduction

The only real way to know about the paranormal is to experience it enough, to read up on it enough, and to start piecing things together. My real wish is that this book gets you to start asking your own questions. There is something out there we don't understand, and haven't since the beginning of time, so maybe the traditional can't answer it. Only fresh eyes can push this forward.

Just please remember to save a little awe in your heart and still get chills when the floors creak in the middle of the night.

PART 1

GETTING TO KNOW
GHOSTS

The word *ghost* conjures up different images for different people. For every person who sees little Casper when he hears about ghosts, there is someone else who has touched the unknown side of the world—and been perplexed by it. Until recently, this confusion was matched only by the lack of information out there. They knew they had experienced something, and they knew there were places in their town everyone said were haunted, but what was it they had seen?

With so much unknown and so much undefined, trying to discover what might be haunting a house is like trying to weigh the human soul or find the color of love. This is made harder when there is so much misinformation out there for people to lean on. Contacting a ghost or talking to the dead is not easy. Although there are people whose job it is to help you do these things, you must start with the basics. Consider the who, what, where, and how of your situation and you'll be off to a good start! If you're lucky, you may get a clue from the other side, but don't forget, ghosts are notoriously mysterious—the why might always remain unanswered.

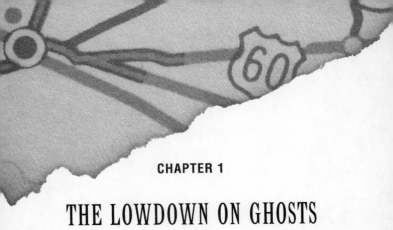

CHAPTER 1

THE LOWDOWN ON GHOSTS

Unless you have already had a firsthand paranormal experience or you believe you have seen or interacted with a ghost, spirit, apparition, or poltergeist, chances are what you are about to read in this book will seem rather bizarre and perhaps a bit scary. The information may also contradict your personal or religious beliefs.

In this chapter, you will receive a general introduction to paranormal activity relating to ghosts and hauntings. Later in the book you will read about professional ghost hunters, paranormal investigators, and people who have experienced paranormal activity. You will learn what to do if you believe you've seen a ghost or experienced paranormal activity yourself, and you will discover places throughout America and around the world where you can visit if you are interested in going on your own real-life paranormal investigation or ghost hunt.

While Hollywood specializes in films like *Poltergeist*, *The Exorcist*, *The Sixth Sense*, and *Ghostbusters* that typically portray ghosts as evil entities that go around scaring and killing people, the real-life paranormal experiences most people report are absolutely nothing like what you see in movies.

As your quest to further understand the paranormal begins, it's important to have a basic understanding of the terms used by the experts to define and describe ghosts, haunts, and other paranormal activity.

Defining Life after Death

According to *Merriam-Webster's Collegiate Dictionary*, 10th edition, a ghost is defined as:

1. the seat of life or intelligence
2. a disembodied soul; the soul of a dead person believed to be an inhabitant of the unseen world or to appear to the living in bodily likeness
3. spirit, demon
4. a faint, shadowy trace
5. a false image in a photographic negative or on a television screen caused by reflection

The definition is a bit limiting, and today so much of the paranormal world lies outside of these lines.

Depending on whom you ask, a ghost is defined in many different ways. To keep things simple, in this book the term *ghost* or *entity* is used to define a wide range of paranormal activity, whether it's an apparition, poltergeist, floating orb of light, or a strange noise emanating from what's believed to be a haunted house or location.

A ghost may in fact be proof of life after death. As you will read in this book, a ghost also can be the result of a strange electrical anomaly that causes what we believe to be paranormal activity but that is not necessarily associated with an entity returning to earth or one that's unable to leave the living realm, for whatever reason, after its death.

The fact is, in today's modern world where science attempts to answer all questions, even without absolute scientific proof, over half of the American and European populations believe in some form of life after death, which includes a belief in ghosts.

The Difference Between Ghosts and Apparitions

What is a ghost? The question seems easy to answer until you begin to look at the evidence people have gathered and the stories witnesses tell. Many people use the word *ghost* to explain the visual appearance of a human being or creature that has died and passed on to the other side. Paranormal experts generally explain this as a visual manifestation of a soul, spirit, life force, or life energy. An *apparition*, on the other hand, typically refers to the visual appearance of any spirit or unusual visual phenomenon that does not necessarily take on the shape of a human form or that does not show signs of intelligence or personality.

All too often, these terms are used interchangeably by nonexperts. In specific terms, however, all ghosts can be considered apparitions, but not all apparitions can be considered ghosts. To keep things interesting, people also use *phantom*, *spook*, *phantasm*, *poltergeist*, or *vision* to describe the visual appearance of a ghost or apparition. The term *collective apparition* is often used to describe an apparition that is seen simultaneously by multiple witnesses.

What Do the Experts Think?

According to one of the world's leading paranormal investigators, Loyd Auerbach, and his Web site (*www .mindreader.com*), apparitions, which are better known as "ghosts," could be some form of the human mind (consciousness, personality, soul, spirit) that functions apart from the physical body. What is believed to be a ghost may be what survives the death of the body. Many reports indicate that apparitions act just like living humans. Some are even believed to have personality and emotions. Many eyewitnesses report that the ghosts they see also act and dress like the people they were when alive. If a woman who lived in eighteenth-century England chooses to return to our realm and be seen as a ghost, she is likely to appear dressed in clothing from eighteenth-century England, not in a modern outfit.

Classifications by Auerbach

Auerbach believes there are five categories of apparitions:

1. *Apparitions of the dead* are people who have been dead for more than twelve to forty-eight hours and who return to visit someone they knew when alive or return to a specific location that's currently inhabited by someone they knew when alive.
2. *Crisis apparitions* are people who have recently died, usually less than twelve hours ago, and often appear with an important message to convey to someone they were close to.
3. *Apparitions of the living,* also referred to as *bilocation*, involve living people having out-of-body experiences.
4. *Apparitions from another dimension or time* are apparitions that visit us from somewhere else or from another time and appear to be as confused and frightened of their visit to our world of the living as the people who witness them.
5. *Pseudo-apparitions* refer to apparitions that actually haunt a location and may create poltergeist phenomena, which involve interactions with the physical environment. These apparitions, according to Auerbach's Web site, do not typically show signs of personality or intelligence. Their actions or the sounds they create are replays of something that has already occurred, and those actions are repeated over and over.

What People See

Some ghosts are visible to the human eye and can take on a variety of different appearances, ranging from a floating cloud of smoke to the three-dimensional image of a human. In many cases, when someone sees a ghost, the ghost displays no intelligence and makes no attempt to interact with the witness(es). It just appears and then disappears, often at the same location over and over again. Some people believe these images have somehow imprinted or attached themselves to a specific location, sort of like a DVR or VCR makes a recording. The image somehow has the ability to keep replaying itself over and over again. This phenomenon is typically classified as an apparition and referred to as a residual haunting. These types of ghosts are the most common form of spirit, but also one of the most frustrating to deal with. They can only be removed from a house or haunted site by disturbing the energy of the location, because they have no living personality you can talk to and help to move on.

Communicating with Ghosts

Many people who report seeing ghosts swear that the entity they encountered communicated with them. Sometimes this communication occurs in a purely visual manner. However, there are also plenty of reports from people who have actually heard a ghost speak to them or who claim to have communicated with a ghost telepathically by exchanging thoughts, not audible words. Any ghost that communicates clearly shows signs of intelligence and often has a specific purpose for making itself known.

Some witnesses of paranormal activity don't see or hear a ghost's presence; instead, they feel it. In some occurrences, the temperature around the witness changes, often dropping dramatically, or an invisible presence is felt physically touching the witness. Some people hear strange noises or simply sense something around them that is not normal.

While some people claim to see or hear ghosts, others have experienced ghosts actually interacting with them or the environment. We will discuss communication with the dead more in Chapter 2.

Crisis Apparitions and Their Messages

There are many ghostly experiences, though, that fall outside the lines of Auerbach's classifications. The haunting may be brief or have some reason or preordained purpose, and as soon as the incident is over, life returns to normal. These incidents offer little proof of life after death, but their effect on those who experience them cannot be ignored.

Crisis apparitions are quite common, and people usually dismiss them until asked if they have ever seen a ghost. A spirit, usually of a loved one or relative, appears to someone at the moment of death or in a time of need. People report seeing an apparition, sometimes as a translucent figure but usually solid, as if it were in the room. Usually, a message is given. The phantom most likely tells the witness things are going to be okay, or it merely says goodbye. Another interesting aspect of this is the crisis phone call, in which a departed spirit uses the phone to give the same type of message.

Not Quite Ghosts—Poltergeists and Other Hauntings

While a ghost is often seen, a poltergeist is more often experienced. A poltergeist will often interact with its environment or with people by moving objects, making noises, or making itself known in other ways. Poltergeists have been reported to be responsible for starting fires, throwing stones, making objects appear and disappear, causing unexplainable sounds, and even levitating physical objects. In fact, the word *poltergeist* means "noisy ghost" when translated from German. Poltergeists typically are not seen.

A poltergeist is also not generally considered to be the spirit of someone who has somehow returned from the dead. Some people believe that poltergeists come from nonhuman origin, while others believe that they are actually living humans with psychic or telekinetic abilities that create this phenomenon. Contrary to popular belief and what's been commonly portrayed in horror movies, poltergeists are not always evil. There have been very few reports of people actually being physically harmed or killed by poltergeists. They are considered by some experts to be more dangerous than ghosts or apparitions. Objects get moved, doors open and close for no reason, or other forms of interaction take place. This type of ghost is typically classified as a poltergeist.

An Explanation for a Poltergeist

According to the book *Ghost Watching* by John Spencer and Tony Wells, the spiritualist explanation for the poltergeist is that occasionally spirits do not leave the earthly plane for their proper place, and for several reasons this may cause disruptive activity. "The main reason for this is that the spirits may be irritated because living people do not recognize them or react to their presence. In their anger they may try to attract attention or simply discharge their aggression by typical poltergeist activity, such as throwing household equipment around. This belief, like all others relating to paranormal activity, is based on faith rather than explicit evidence." This is just one possible theory regarding the origin of poltergeists.

Telekinetic Energy and Poltergeist Hauntings

The dominant theory involves the telekinetic energy of someone in the house. Many believe the energy produced by some trauma may be strong enough to physically move things. Most cases involve a youth in a critical stage of development, such as puberty or late adolescence. Often the child in the house has suffered some type of abuse—physical, psychological, or sexual—and many times the abuser is the focus of the attacks.

Shadow People

While reports of shadow people are nothing new, sightings of these elusive spirits are coming out now more than ever. These sightings are a question mark in the field, rarely photographed and never recorded. Their purpose is as difficult to determine as what they are.

There are several physical descriptions of shadow people, and it is hard to classify them as ghosts or something more evil, like demons. Most of the time, they are said to be made of thick, black fog, but they're solid, so you could touch them and not have your hand go through them. While they sometimes are seen as only masses, they usually appear in the form of a person, which the witness always describes as a negative, male presence. Usually the full body is seen, and the face is either a void or only red eyes. They have been known to be small, about three to four feet, but more often than not, people report visions that are taller than six feet and of muscular build.

No one has been able to nail down exactly what they are, but most people agree that they are most often seen observing the living. They live in the corners of rooms and mirrors and are spotted out of the corner of the observer's eye, never making contact but watching.

When Do Shadow People Appear?

Shadow people are spotted most often in places where there is other paranormal activity, and they act as witnesses to what is happening. Many people report having a ghost and living with the haunting, but then another dark spirit comes into the house. Investigators called in to investigate a haunting or explore a known haunted area will tell stories of how they were watched by a dark figure who stepped behind walls or vanished behind a tree.

Shadow people also find their way to places of extreme emotion. They have been spotted in cemeteries, even those that are no longer in use. They have been reported in prisons and hospitals as well as mental health hospitals, even after the places have closed or are not in use anymore.

The actions of shadow people lead some in the field to believe that they feed off energy. Not quite demons, or at least not classified as traditional demons, they might get their strength from the sadness or fear of the living, or from the energy of the other spirits. They never want to communicate, only to be there.

Defining Doppelgangers

Doppelgangers are often misunderstood, and their meaning has been changed through the years. Most people believe a doppelganger to be someone living who looks exactly like someone else. Both are independent people. In the world of the paranormal, the phrase actually refers to seeing yourself. The experience is said to be a glimpse into the moment of one's own death. Seeing your doppelganger is rare, but there are stories of people seeing themselves while fully awake doing something. Everything else is normal; they just view another version of themselves doing something. They tell the story to someone close, not able to make sense of what they have seen, and sometime after that, they die while doing what they had reportedly seen. While not all sightings revolve around the death of the person, they almost always are connected to horrific experiences, almost as if they are warnings of what's to come.

The're All Around You—Even in Your Dreams

Dreams are usually discounted when it comes to the paranormal, but they offer some of the best firsthand evidence of ghosts. While it is difficult to put too much weight into people seeing something unexplained while they are sleeping, when what they dream is backed up with other evidence, it becomes harder to mark the dream as a coincidence. Dreams are often the precursors to other hauntings.

Dreams are hardly proof, but ghosts may be able to use them to communicate. Our waking minds may be too closed off to accept the idea of something unseen in our houses, but our dreaming, subconscious minds may be just open enough for them to get through.

Time Slips

Many believe the universe works on different dimensions, and at times those worlds can open up and show themselves to us. Some believe ghosts are just people who have slipped through this veil and, for one reason or another, temporarily become part of this world. Sometimes the gate swings the other way, and someone from this world travels to another place for a brief time. In this situation, which almost always involves a vision of the past, the experiencer is the ghost. These are called time slips, and they have been reported throughout history. Sometimes people can interact with the people they see, but usually they are merely observers. Although most involve historical places, some are seen in places of immense energy released by a traumatic event.

What Does a Near-Death Experience Teach You?

Near-death experiences (NDEs) occur to people all over the world, mostly to people who have a solid belief in ghosts. Why include them in a book about ghosts? The events of an NDE are very real for those who suffer through them, and the way they view the world and the beings they interact with point at a possible afterlife. These experiences may be the place where the spirit can be trapped, the gateway to where the soul goes when the body dies. That path is worth exploring.

People who have experienced an NDE are not necessarily religious, interested in the paranormal, or gifted with psychic abilities. Many lead normal lives until their experience, which they later describe as life-changing. Almost everyone who has experienced an NDE describes seeing a bright light that is all-encompassing. One of the things that make this phenomenon more credible to the average skeptic than other types of paranormal events is that the people who experience an NDE often do not claim to possess some magical or supernatural power. They have nothing to gain from discussing their experience, and often run the risk of being labeled a freak or nut case.

What to Expect from an NDE

Based on research conducted, some of the common experiences during an NDE include:

- The "self" leaving the body and hovering overhead
- Travel through a dark area, sometimes described as a tunnel
- Extremely powerful emotions, sometimes described as pure bliss and other times described as frightening
- A golden, white light that the experiencer can look into without hurting his or her eyes
- A message encouraging the experiencer to turn back from the light because it is not his time yet

- A meeting and/or communication with deceased loved ones
- A sighting of a sacred being or religious leader
- Reliving highlights from the person's life
- A brief instant of understanding how the universe works
- A barrier or obstacle that keeps the person from proceeding and forces him to turn back (some people believe that they are given a choice and asked if they wish to return to the living)

Overall, many people describe NDEs as being extremely pleasant, experiences that totally eliminate any fear of death. Some people, however, report having experiences that are frightening.

Channelers and Psychics Help You Communicate

Millions of people believe that those who have died live on in an afterlife and can choose to communicate with the living, often through someone who seems to have otherworldly powers. Throughout history, cultures from around the world have believed that the living could communicate with the dead. This is evident among cultures from ancient Egypt, China, and Greece, for example, and in many religions worldwide.

Some people believe they have the ability to communicate freely with the dead. These people are called mediums or channelers. While some are frauds, unscrupulously preying on the emotional needs of the public, others have a gift that they believe allows them to communicate directly with ghosts or spirits, and these people continue to defy scientific belief and demonstrate their abilities.

Unfortunately, many of the people who choose to use the services of a channeler or medium in order to communicate with a deceased loved one are often experiencing a strong sense of grief, depression, anxiety, or desperation and are easily manipulated or duped by highly skilled con artists. People who offer their gift to others in exchange for little or no financial compensation are often the most credible since these people have nothing to gain.

Typically a channeler or a medium is used to assist someone in communicating with someone who is deceased. For this communication to take place, the medium or channeler must make contact with the spirit or ghost of someone who has died and who is believed to now exist within the spiritual plane, which perhaps is heaven or the place where spirits go after death. This place is often referred to as the spirit world or the other side.

A spirit or ghost that uses a medium in order to communicate with someone either verbally or visually is known as a *spirit communicator*. Likewise, a spirit or ghost that uses a medium to physically manipulate something on earth is referred to as a *spirit operator*.

How the Communication Works

The spirit or ghost can communicate with a medium or channeler in a number of ways, often involving some form of mental telepathy. The medium typically then verbally communicates with the living people around him or her to pass along messages from the deceased. It is the medium, not the living witnesses, who sees, hears, feels, or senses what the spirit or ghost is trying to communicate. A medium's responsibility is to communicate whatever message the deceased person is attempting to relay without any personal interference.

No matter where you travel in the world, people who call themselves shamans, witch doctors, wise men or wise women, clairvoyants, clairaudients, psychics, channelers, or mediums can be found. For some reason these people are able to harness the power of the mind and the energy around them in ways others cannot in order to communicate with the spirit world. While everyone has basic intuition, people who are able to harness their psychic abilities and communicate with the other side have found ways to tap their sixth sense and open their minds to higher levels of consciousness.

Do You Believe in Reincarnation?

Do you believe that when living beings die they can come back to the world as another living being? The Center for Human Relations suggests that the overall concept of reincarnation involves the possibility of embodiment and re-embodiment of the eternal spirit, the continuation of the soul consciousness, from one physical lifetime to the next physical lifetime in a human body.

Based on its research, the center reports, "During the course of a human lifetime, the essence of human interaction is often misperceived and misinterpreted then compared with past memories. The conscious mind, or ego, develops false assumptions, draws base-less conclusions, makes faulty judgments and survival-based decisions, all of which are inappropriate to the current situation. These errors of mind, or the mental residue, pervert the interactions with other people and lead to emotional residues of anger and resentment, fear, sadness and loss, guilt and remorse, distortions of love and the pain of unrequited or lost love."

A Space Between Lives

Assuming you believe in reincarnation and that as living beings we have the ability to experience mul-tiple lifetimes, what happens to us or our spirits in between those lifetimes? The Center for Human Rela-tions explains that in the spirit space between lives, sometimes called the Light, there is a Planning Stage. This is where conditions are designed for the coming physical lifetime. It is believed that prior to embodi-ment, the beings involved in past interactions work together to develop situations that will allow for the resolution of their residues and the evolvement of inner peace and harmony.

After a being becomes enmeshed in a new lifetime, the greater spiritual reality is somehow forgotten. The planned situations then arise, and free will allows for choices to be made during that lifetime. The center hypothesizes that some choices lead to resolution and growth. Other choices lead to fear, perpetuation of the conflict, and persistence and aggravation of the residues. There is no judgment of right or wrong involved in these choices. The outcome affects only those who make the choices.

It is believed that all memories acquired during all of our lifetimes are stored in our subconscious minds. When someone experiences past-life regression, what is experienced can have many meanings.

Your Psychic Ability

There is a bit of a psychic in us all. Some have trained that part of themselves to hear what others cannot, but the skill lies within each person searching for the truth. Most times we do not want it to work. We wish we did not have that quick leap in our stomachs in the dark, that moment of pause that tells us something is there. We spend most of our lives telling ourselves we are not sensitive, and that feeling we have that we are not alone is merely a figment of our imaginations, not something we could touch if we gave into our other mind.

Those who experience the paranormal often need to tap into their psychic abilities to help explain what is happening to them. Regardless whether you ask for professional help or build your own skills, it can be the ticket outside the normal.

The Dark Side

There is a dark side to the paranormal that goes beyond just the fear we might have toward ghosts. Spirits, for the most part, cannot hurt you, but there are other things investigators come upon that can do harm to individuals and families. They are a danger to investigators because they hide in between ghosts and are slow to make themselves known. They can look and sound and feel like a run-of-the-mill spirit, if there is such a thing. These demons, not of this world but always present, are to be feared and respected and not challenged. They try to attach themselves to people and houses, and their intentions are never positive. Some investigators feel many hauntings have something darker waiting in the wings.

An Expert's Opinion on the Dark Side

Keith Johnson is the founder of New England Anomalies Research and a demonologist. He has worked with the Atlantic Paranormal Society (TAPS) and New England Paranormal and is sought after for his knowledge in the field of demons and other inhuman spirits. He has been busy lately as both an investigator and as a resource for other ghost hunters who find themselves face to face with something they think might be a demon. Johnson offers counseling to people over the Internet and over the phone. His Web site (*www.nearparanormal.com*) invites people to decide for themselves if they may have a manifestation and gives advice for those who believe a demon has entered their lives.

According to Johnson, there are different types of nonhuman spirits, the most powerful of which are demons. In his years looking into demonic attacks, spanning over forty cases, he has seen what they have to offer and feels most infestations are a crime of opportunity. A demon's ultimate goal is the distortion of anything godly and the corrupting of the human spirit.

The higher-level, leader demons don't like to reveal themselves, but they control a number of lesser spirits and give them energy. The lesser demons are almost animal-like and are the ones who generally take part in trying to possess people. Johnson believes that all paranormal occurrences have the potential for demons to get involved because interest creates an opening or an access point for dark spirits. About a third of the cases he has investigated have had some type of demonic influence.

Getting More Than You Bargained for

While there are cases where a person or group invites a demon into their lives, generally a person falls victim through an innocent mistake. Many demons hide as another, more romantic element of the paranormal. Someone might be left open because the person has experimented with unorthodox religions or has an interest in the occult, and many demonologists feel intense negative activities invite the demonic. The most common approach is through a minor haunting or by making communication through a device such as a Ouija board or even during an electronic voice phenomena (EVP) session. Your interest in the supernatural attracts them, and the communication serves to make you open to them. By engaging the other side, you give up a part of your mind and body to something you cannot see and cannot control. Anything can come through. Once they have that opening, they enter your life and go about making your home theirs.

During an Infestation

The demons give signs they are something inhuman, but most people who experience them cannot tell the difference. They favor the left side and like to do things in threes. For example, a ghost might rap on the wall to tell you she is there, but a demon might knock three times at three in the morning. Demons also have a strength not seen in human spirits. They have the ability to move larger objects and even physically assault people.

When an infestation happens, an inhuman spirit can latch on and notify other spirits of the fertile breeding ground. Higher-level demons, always in contact and control of their minions, also find chances to feed, making the manifestation worse. They set up shop and ask you to talk to them more often and demand more from you. One of the telltale signs of an infestation is when the demon constantly demands the victim be alone and isolated from others. Talking to the spirit becomes the center of a person's day. A demonic attack has two main stages, and this is the first, appropriately named obsession.

The Obsession Turns Intense

Imagine the worst kind of haunting, and then imagine it happening on a constant basis. Some of the most frightening episodes involve hearing low and guttural voices and seeing full-bodied, solid apparitions. Once the demon has a foothold, it will work to isolate the subject from all positive supports in his family. The goal is to make the subject too weak to resist and to potentially possess the other family members as well. The attacks become too much for the family. When the person or the family is at their lowest, when they see no other way out or cannot fight anymore, the demon can move in. All of this combat is to prepare the person for possession, or complete control.

For some the progression of possession is rapid, but other times people exist in obsession for some time. Most times in possession the victim is in what is called a transient state. The demon comes and goes at will but only for brief periods of time. Most of the time the person is lucid and unaware he has fallen into a possessed state, although during those times he will do horrible things he does not remember. The possessed person might report blackouts and feeling outside of himself. He reacts violently to religious provocation and will strike out against it as the demon cannot take the words anymore. In perfect possession, a term coined by the late Father Malachi Martin, the demon is always upfront.

The Confrontation

In either of the levels, the demon must be challenged and dealt with, although this is not advisable for the average person. The traditional view has been that only a Roman Catholic priest, with the blessing of the Roman Catholic Church, can conduct an exorcism, although in recent years many religions have given this power to others. The person best suited to do this battle is someone trained in his religion and not a part-time ghost hunter. Demonologists, while well versed in different aspects of the religion, often do not feel prepared to conduct the ritual themselves when the victim has moved beyond the obsession stage. That is best left to professional clergy.

A demonologist can do quite a bit before the demon takes full control. Johnson says the most effective defense against an infestation is praying and spreading positive feelings. He does both when he conducts an investigation and realizes he is dealing with a demonic presence. After a blessing, many of the problems in the house can be put to rest, but there is always a chance that the demon can return if the family allows it in again.

CHAPTER 2

INVESTIGATING THE OTHER SIDE

Investigating the paranormal is about finding a haunted place and knowing what to do when you get there. While there may be places where you live that are known to be haunted, a ghost can make its home anywhere. An investigator must learn what to look for, how to gather evidence, and how to communicate with the dead. One of the engaging aspects of the paranormal is you can determine your level of involvement in research. Some investigators sometimes find things following them home or have a darker element entering into their work. For the most part, mistakes out in the field are more about lack of knowledge than any harm a phantom can do to you. A well thought out plan and an understanding of the equipment you use is perhaps your best tool.

Finding the Ghosts Yourself

An investigation is about getting evidence, which can be gathered in different ways. It is important to know what to look for and how to tell what kind of spirit you may be encountering. When many people think of a ghost, the image in their minds is of a human form that is somewhat translucent or that glows in the dark or floats in the air. These full-bodied apparitions are rarely seen when you want to see them. Most investigators look more for ghosts that appear as floating balls of light or as orbs of energy.

What Can You Catch on Film?

According to Janis Raley, cofounder of the Ghost Preservation League, a group of professional and amateur paranormal investigators, by far the most common phenomenon caught on film is of an orb or sphere. "We have seen some that look like small bubbles, cinnamon buns, and a bad case of the hives. They can occur as single orbs, in clusters, in whirling clumps, be bright as stars, or be barely visible. They can look radically different but are recognizable as the same general type of phenomena," she says.

What are these orbs that are captured on film? Some people insist they are trapped souls.

Mist and vapor are other forms of energy that some believe to have paranormal origins and are often seen on investigations. According to Raley, they accompany, or cause, cold spots. Much of the equipment mentioned later in this chapter will focus on measuring these temperature changes, but some are strong enough to be noticed by our natural senses.

Aside from orbs and vapors, forces known as "vortices" are a very concentrated form of energy. These forces are often described as the kind that causes the hair on the back of your neck to stand at attention. A vortex is a mass of air, water, or, in this case, energy that spins around very fast and pulls objects into its empty center. Some believe that energy-based vortices have paranormal origins. Those who incorporate some type of quantum physics into their belief system believe these represent the crossing point between two different worlds or realities. Ghosts might float between these, and finding one on film represents an entry point.

Where to Look

Spirits can be found anywhere. Ghosts have been reported to appear or manifest themselves in many different locations, not just places where something evil or tragic has taken place, such as the site of a murder, suicide, or battle. Some experts equate ghosts, hauntings, and other paranormal activity with unusual energy fields located at specific locations. These energy fields might be natural, perhaps a result of metal deposits in the ground, a fault, or an underground water supply, or they might be the result of faulty electrical wiring in a house.

While it has been scientifically proven that many haunted locations are often in close proximity to electrical, magnetic, or geomagnetic energy fields, the exact correlation between the ghosts and these energy fields has yet to be determined. Some believe the electrical, geomagnetic, or magnetic energy fields open a doorway or create a portal that allows ghosts to make themselves known. Still others believe it is the ghosts themselves create the anomaly or cause the unusual energy field. Others say the waves have an effect on the observer and cause a more open, accepting mind.

Whether or not you believe that electrical, geomagnetic, or magnetic energy fields have any relationship to the presence and manifestation of ghosts, apparitions, paranormal entities, or poltergeists, there are many types of locations where these phenomena have been documented to take place.

Popular Haunted Places

Some of the most popular places where ghosts seem apt to make themselves known include:

- Battlefields
- Cemeteries
- Crime scenes
- Sites of suicides
- Older educational institutions
- Homes
- Hospitals and asylums
- Jails and prisons

- Hotels, motels, and inns
- Nursing homes
- Theaters

One of the best ways of finding haunted locations is to do research. Pay careful attention to local folklore. Research as much as possible the origins of that folklore and be aware of similar myths being spread in other communities. The majority of these locations have strange events or unusual stories associated with them. The best piece of equipment an investigator has is a library card.

The Ghost Hunting Toolbox

One of the crucial things TAPS did was to bring equipment to the forefront of an investigation. No longer was the sensitive person the leader of a group. Now the techie ran things and reached into his toolbox for the right equipment. Most of the tools can be bought at any number of local stores or online and include the following:

Air ion counter: This device can be used to detect natural and artificial ions. Natural ions have explanations, but it's been documented by researchers that ghosts tend to either create ion fields or alter the ion fields in a location where they manifest themselves.

Audio recorder: A cassette, DAT, or Minidisc audio recorder can be used to record electronic voice phenomena (EVP), and some have even used the audio track of a common video recorder to gather audio evidence.

Compass: You can purchase several different pieces of equipment to detect magnetic or electromagnetic fields, but a simple hand-held compass is a low-tech way of measuring this type of energy anomaly.

Electromagnetic field (EMF) Gauss meter: This device can be used to detect and measure electromagnetic fields and electrical current located within an area that is believed to be haunted.

Geiger counter: Paranormal investigators use this device to check the background radiation that is present at a specific location. If ghosts are, in fact, energy based, this tool, which measures certain types of energy that may be present at the site of a haunting, may detect them.

Infrared proximity detector: This device is used to detect even the slightest movements in an area by measuring changes in temperature and light.

Magnetic field detector: This device pinpoints and measures the presence of low-level magnetic fields, which are often associated with ghosts and paranormal activity.

Notebook and pen/pencil: As you're participating in an investigation, even if it's in your own home, document in as much detail as possible everything you experience.

Temperature-reading equipment: Sudden temperature changes have long been associated with poltergeist phenomena. Being able to take ongoing temperature readings of an area will help you document these changes and possibly alert you to paranormal activity that's taking place but that is not visible to the human eye.

Stopwatch: In addition to having a wristwatch or clock, a stopwatch is extremely useful for measuring and documenting how long a paranormal activity lasts.

Sugar or salt or flour: By sprinkling salt or sugar around objects, such as furniture, where a ghost might move, you can easily determine if movement has taken place based on how the sugar or salt is scattered around the object. This is a very low-tech alternative to using a motion detector.

Crosses or other religious objects: Although these types of investigations are based in science, many investigators still carry items born of the old traditions. Some carry holy water or incense, believing such things can protect them or draw spirits out.

These are totally at the discretion of the investigator and are unique to his or her belief system.

Voice stress analyzer: When it comes to interviewing witnesses who claim to have experienced or witnessed paranormal activity, not everyone will be reliable. To help determine if someone is lying, a voice stress analyzer can be used.

Photography

A picture is worth a thousand words, and photography is essential in gathering evidence at a location. People who do not believe ghosts are real will still look twice at a picture or a video showing something that cannot be explained away. Amateur and professional paranormal investigators alike use a wide range of photographic equipment, including 35mm cameras, basic point-and-shoot cameras, and Polaroid instant cameras. Video camcorders and digital cameras are also used in an attempt to document paranormal activity. Obviously, you'll want to use the best equipment possible. If you're using a traditional camera, be sure to have plenty of 400 ASA or faster speed film. Faster film speeds allow you to take better pictures of fast-moving objects and to photograph in low light. Digital cameras are often the tool of choice and are becoming cheaper to use, though recently there has been a backlash against them. Digital cameras seem to record more orbs and mists. Advocates say this is because digital cameras photograph on a broader spectrum of light and can pick up more than the human eye or traditional cameras. Others say the orbs represent a flaw in the cameras and lessen the impact of visual evidence.

Talking to the Dead

No matter how you choose to attempt contact with the spirit world, whether it's through past-life regression, channeling, use of a medium (psychic), use of a Ouija board, a pendulum, tarot cards, or any other fortune-telling tool, take whatever information you learn to heart, but do not allow this information to control your life. Everyone is born with free will. The information you believe you obtain from the other side can be used to console you, counsel you, or educate you, but it should not be used to dictate every action you take in life.

When participating in any activities that involve the paranormal, always proceed with caution, taking action only after you have carefully and thoroughly educated yourself. Just as you would not make jokes to someone who is highly religious about his or her belief system, tapping your own abilities to contact the spirit world should be for your personal growth, not for entertainment purposes.

The Ouija Board Speaks

While sitting in the comfort of one's own home, many believe it is possible to establish a connection with the other side using a talking board or a channeling board, more commonly known today as a Ouija board. The concept behind a Ouija board is rather simple. It is typically a board or flat surface with each letter of the alphabet, the numbers zero through nine, and the words *yes* and *no* printed on it. Using a small pointing device called a planchette, psychics, mediums, and others experimenting with paranormal phenomena can use this tool in an attempt to summon a spirit and ask it questions. The person (or people) using the Ouija board keeps the tips of his or her fingers lightly touching the planchette so that it can freely move around the Ouija board as if guided by a spirit or paranormal energy. Many believe that once communication with the other side begins, the questions people ask are answered by the spirits, who make the person's hand move the planchette around the Ouija board in order to spell out words or simply answer yes or no to questions.

How to Use the Board Effectively

True believers in the power of the Ouija board feel it is the power of the subconscious mind that allows users to tap into the other side and make contact with spirits. The typical use of this tool involves two people facing each other with the board between them and their fingers lightly touching the planchette. When used correctly, the planchette will begin to move without consciously being controlled by those touching it. After a question is asked of the spirit(s), the planchette should move from one letter to the next and ultimately spell out an answer, or it will point to the yes or no areas of the board.

Those who have experienced the use of a Ouija board have mixed interpretations of their experiences. Some believe the board takes on a life of its own, working as a message carrier from the other side. Others see it as nothing more than a game that provides harmless entertainment, just like Monopoly, chess, checkers, or backgammon.

Operator's Instructions

If you're so inclined to experience using a Ouija board, here is how to operate it. Have two or more people sit facing each other. Place the board on the knees of the individuals or on a small table placed between the two people. Those involved should then gently place their fingers, without using any pressure, upon the planchette, which should be placed near the center of the board. The people actually touching the planchette should allow it to move freely, allowing the spirit or whatever the driving force is to move the object without the conscious mind of the operator being involved.

Let the planchette sit with fingers upon it for several minutes as the users sit quietly and focus their minds on a single question. After one to five minutes, ask a question out loud. The planchette should begin to move, traveling from letter to letter or number on the Ouija board as it spells out the answer to the question at hand. Individual words, phrases, full sentences, or yes or no answers may result from the planchette's moving. It should be understood that the planchette might spell out abbreviated words or use symbolic messages. Be sure to have someone looking on to write down all of the messages communicated from the session. Messages might not make sense right away. Wait until the session is over, and then review everything that was received in terms of words and phrases.

Tips to Ensure the Best Results

During the process, only one question should be asked at a time, and all questions should be stated clearly. Once the question is asked, everyone involved, including onlookers, should clear her mind and focus only on the question being asked. Some psychics believe that the Ouija board should never be used to answer frivolous or ridiculous questions, as this could anger the spirits.

Experts using this fortune-telling tool recommend that the room where the Ouija board is being used be kept quiet, with no nearby distractions of any kind. Those who have become skilled at using this tool explain that it takes practice to become proficient, just as it does when learning how to ride a bicycle. The first time you attempt to use this tool, don't become frustrated if nothing amazing happens. Simply clear your mind and keep trying.

A Warning about the Board

There is a darker side though, as many people have had negative experiences with boards. Ouija boards are like bad drugs. The fix is immediate, the effect is short-lived, and you take a chance every time you use them. People who use the board on a regular basis often find it consumes their lives. They sit down, use it, and soon four hours have gone by. There is also a threat of possession. Demons look for any entrance. Many demonic attacks have begun with use of the board.

The abbreviations and cryptic answers the board gives can be a spirit's way of keeping you around. Many feel the spirit, whether it be human or demon, feeds off the user's energy. The longer it can keep you on, the more it can feed. The information it gives is designed to draw you in and keep you with your fingers on the planchette.

Pendulums and Automatic Writing

In addition to Ouija boards, another common tool, particularly useful for obtaining yes or no answers to your questions, is the pendulum. These work on the idea that the pendulum is an antenna that can pick up energy given off by ghosts in the area. Some people believe that the pendulum can create a bridge between the logical and intuitive parts of the mind. It is also believed that this type of tool can connect the user with a higher power, allowing for information to be communicated from a divine source. There is also a theory that a pendulum simply responds to electromagnetic energy that radiates from everything on earth. Just as with most other tools for communicating with spirits, nobody knows exactly how or why they work, yet many who have used pendulums swear they do work. Once you have obtained a pendulum, here is how to use it:

1. Still the pendulum by holding it in the air from its chain or string, using your thumb and index finger.
2. Say out loud, "Show me YES." This should cause the pendulum to swing in one direction—for example, from side to side, back and forth, or in circles.
3. After again making the pendulum still, say out loud, "Show me NO." This should cause the pendulum to swing in the opposite direction from a yes response.
4. Repeat these steps several times until you consistently receive the same yes and no responses from the pendulum.
5. Once you are familiar with how your particular pendulum operates, steady the pendulum once again, then ask your question. When the pendulum starts to move again, it should reveal the answer you seek.

What Is Automatic Writing?

Using nothing but a pen and paper, some mediums believe they can relax their minds and bodies until spirits take control of their hands and start writing or drawing with them. This process is called automatic writing or inspirational writing and involves putting your mind in a receptive state, much as you would when contacting a spirit guide, and using a pen and paper to write down or draw whatever messages or images come to mind.

The process is done without your conscious mind actually thinking about what's being written or drawn on the page. It involves free association and capturing as much information as possible on paper. The information that is communicated through your hand onto the paper may be in the form of single words, phrases, sentences, entire pages of text, images, drawings, paintings, or symbols.

A Helpful Web Site

The Healing from Within Web site (*www.healing fromwithin.com/Articles/Automatic_Writing/automatic_ writing.html*) provides information about an easy exercise anyone can do to experiment with this process. Begin by following these steps:

1. Find a quiet place and make yourself comfortable.
2. Have a pen and pad of paper ready.

3. At the top of the piece of paper, write down what you would like guidance on. You can seek out general advice or ask a very specific question. Some experts suggest also writing the date at the top of the paper.

4. Using meditation, spend a few minutes relaxing and clearing your conscious mind. This is often referred to as centering yourself. Pay careful attention to your breathing and take several slow, deep breaths. Allow your mind and body to relax.

Once your mind is relaxed and open to the opportunity of communicating with your inner self or a spirit from the other side, seek out the guidance you need by asking for it.

"Do not judge, analyze, or evaluate what you have written even if it does not answer your question. Write until your hand is done. When you are finished read what you wrote," explains The Healing from Within Web site.

Some companies have even created a device to help you in your writing. Most look like a Ouija board planchette, only with some writing device in the middle. As with any form of communication with the other side, it is not clear if the messages received through automatic writing are actually coming from a spirit that you are channeling or if it's only your subconscious mind at work. Obviously, people interpret this phenomenon and the results from it in different ways.

Electronic Voice Phenomena

Electronic voice phenomena (EVP) are the noises and voices that are recorded on traditional audio or video-tape but are not audible to the human ear prior to being recorded. Karen Mossey, an expert in the field of EVPs and a founding member of the East Coast Transcom-munication Organization (ECTO, *www.ectoweb.com*), goes a bit further in her definition. She defines EVP as "the appearance of some type of intelligence that manifests on a recording device that has no physical source we can discover. These voices are a product or originate from people who have died." For research-ers, it is the most real evidence someone can get.

A measurement on an EMF detector or a Geiger counter can be disputed, but a voice on a tape when no one was present is more concrete. Many who work with EVPs describe experiencing the same pull when they heard their first recording. It is the source of many investigators' belief that ghosts exist. It makes the unknown tangible.

How EVPs Work

The scientific idea behind what an EVP might be makes more sense than some of the concepts being thrown around the field today. If ghosts are energy, they might be able to manipulate devices and speak through them or become imprinted on them. Reasons for why it works vary. Most believe there is a range of sound our ears cannot pick up but that can be trapped by recording devices. Spirits can reach out to anyone, meaning a place does not have to be haunted to produce a voice. Many times a ghost will seek out someone to talk to, and if that communication means revealing itself to a person trying to tape voices, that is the path the ghost will take.

Ideas also vary on the best recorder to use. Mossey believes the best recorder is an analog recorder that creates internal noise, such as the sound of the reels spinning. "Entities aren't working with vocal cords or anything physical. They are working with electromagnetic waves, ambient noise within the device itself, and your own physical energy. We have found the lesser-quality recorders have a tendency to work better. They usually have a lower sample rate and produce more noise. I believe it's the noise within these recording devices they are using to record their messages," she says.

Others feel that the better the recorder, the better the results. This usually means using digital, which also is easier to archive and work with. Mike Markowicz, an EVP specialist from East Bridgewater, Massachusetts, uses ten highly sensitive microphones and an entire computer system to get his results. Much of his work is in postproduction, cleaning out the information he gets and watching computer readouts on the nature of the sound waves. Regardless of the process, the result is the same.

What the Skeptics Say

Skeptics say EVPs are not evidence at all but rather proof that mass-marketed technology is better and stronger than we think. They point to radio waves, always present in the air, and say these devices pick up voices from the air, not the other side. Those that work with EVPs point to them as the evidence that will finally convince people there is life after death.

Mossey also believes the spirits want to work with the researcher, but that in many cases there is not an understanding of how to do it. The ghosts want to communicate, but they have no understanding of their own physical abilities. She helps the spirits along by telling them what she is doing when she records and encourages them to use her equipment to talk. She claims 40 percent of her recordings are interactive and talk directly to her or about her. In addition to having her direct questions answered, she has been sworn at and had her name called.

What Can EVPs Record?

EVPs can record residual hauntings as well as direct communication. Mossey, for example, has recorded the voice of her father, who was a local politician, several times. His recordings have often involved his spirit still trying to pass laws and conduct town meetings. While most people who work with EVPs are hard-evidence types of people, Markowicz is different. He believes the energy is not electromagnetic or biome-chanical but rather spiritual. Without a vocal cord or a mouth to produce sound, the energy must come from the soul. For him, the device is irrelevant, and intention is what makes the recording.

Working with EVPs

There are several ways to get good EVPs, and several should be experimented with to get results. The techniques are a reflection of the people who record them. The most common way to get something is to start recording and leave the recorder alone. You may ask questions to try and prompt answers, especially because a direct response makes for better evidence. Researchers ask spirits what their names are, whether they are present, or whether they want to talk. Some feel that they need to provoke the spirits by asking questions that will produce an emotional response.

Matt Moniz, the cohost of a paranormal radio show called *Spooky Southcoast*, has another approach. He asks mundane questions like what their favorite color is, or what kind of music they like. He feels these questions create a rapport with the spirit and may offer answers he can later verify. Mossey suggests doubling up on equipment, mainly because she feels the spirits cannot manipulate two devices at once, and a noise picked up on two recorders is most likely natural. If something is on one recording and not the other, you have stronger proof you have something unseen, and unheard by the human ear. She recommends bringing analog and digital recorders to get the range of both technologies.

After the recording has been made, most investigators run the evidence through audio software to clean it up and isolate anything found on the tape. They also add effects, which, while producing a clearer voice, may also damage the credibility of the evidence. Some even run the EVPs backwards to see if the noises picked up may sound intelligible if played in reverse.

New Technology, New Opportunities

Many times, ghosts have found ways to talk using common household devices. The paranormal field has reported countless times in which a television, a radio, or a computer has allowed some presence to come through. People have even received calls from the dead or messages on their answering machines.

While many investigators are satisfied using the tools that are out there for them now, many are going beyond the normal means to create their own devices for talking and capturing proof of life after death. They try to take the equipment they have and stretch its uses or use existing equipment for a different use. Karen Mossey has been known to place her recorder in a microwave to get better results. While this is not an advisable method, she has gotten voices by doing this. Josh Montello of the Berkshire Paranormal Group has experimented with ultraviolet light, instead of the traditional infrared, with mixed results. Researchers in England are using the empty frequencies in between radio stations to hear other worlds. Each has his own reason for shaking things up.

Television Communication

For all our dependence on the television, we know little about how it works. It can be used to entertain and inform, but some are adapting it to try to talk to spirits, and it has proven to be one of the more reliable and impressive techniques. In the first method, an investigator turns the television on a channel that does not come in. By tuning into static and using the white noise, investigators believe they feed the natural energy a ghost may have and give it a means to talk. The researcher then communicates with the television much like during an EVP session, asking questions and giving whatever is on the other side prompts. The session is best when taped and reviewed later. People have been known to get voices, and at times the screen even reveals a quick face. This kind of communication was explored in *White Noise*, and although the movie was fiction, others have received stunning results.

The second method is a bit more controversial, but some claim to have received many messages from the dead using it. A video camera is set up and pointed at a television screen. The camera is then hooked up to the television, and the tape is left running. What you have is an infinite loop of the image of the screen showing the screen. The science behind why this should work is sketchy. Some have said the loop creates a disturbance in the flow of energy, creating an opening for the ghost.

The Spiricom

When George Meek died in 1999, he left a legacy people are still trying to duplicate today. He created a device known as the Spiricom. According to Jeff

Belanger, noted author, lecturer, and founder of the Web's largest and most popular supernatural community (*www.ghostvillage.com*), "the machine was comprised of tone and frequency generators that emitted thirteen tones in the range of an adult man's voice. When Meek spoke to the spirit world through his machine, the spirit world spoke back by interacting with the tone generators to make recognizable speech. Meek was astounded at his breakthrough." Meek made contact with a scientist who had died a decade earlier and who supposedly helped him fine-tune the machine. They carried on a two-way conversation for many years, with the spirit often coming over the recordings very clearly while other times his voice was muddled. Clips of the conversations, as well as plans for the machine, are all over the Internet.

Over the years the machine has been re-created and modified. While none of these machines has ever reached the results of the original, people still push on using Meek's design. Markowicz has also been working on his own form of the Spiricom using tubing and microphones.

Frank's Box

The most exciting and galvanizing advance in spirit communication has been the development of Frank's box, or the ghost box. The device is named after its original inventor, Frank Sumption, a researcher who was recording EVPs and found the software he was using to edit them had a remarkable glitch. The machine has a white noise generator that runs through circuits and eventually an AM radio receiver. Stations are scanned, and a channel is opened for anything to communicate through. The results were remarkable, and Sumption made his plans and the machine itself available to others. His original intention was to allow as many researchers as possible to use the design and test it in real-world paranormal investigations, as well as to have other technicians make improvements on his ideas. He has since taken the information down and works only with select investigators, but others are taking up the search.

Chris Moon, the editor of *The Haunted Times,* was one of the original people to work with Sumption, but since then he has struck out on his own. He has said he has contacted Thomas Edison on the machine and receives instructions from him. He once claimed Edison said only a limited number of people were allowed to use the machine, but Moon has since retracted that statement. He has used his box at such famously haunted locations as the Lizzie Borden Bed and Breakfast. One of the interesting aspects of Moon's box is that there is heightened paranormal activity during its use. EMF readings spike in other parts of the room, and pictures taken while it is in use have shown clear orbs and other unexplained anomalies. It is difficult to say whether this is due to a higher level of energy created by the machine itself or whether ghosts find the easiest way to talk and are drawn to it.

Enlisting the Help of a Ghost Hunter

A ghost hunter or paranormal investigator is someone who investigates and studies ghosts, hauntings, and paranormal phenomena. A ghost buster, on the other hand, is someone who visits a site that's believed to be haunted and uses any of a wide range of methods to eliminate the ghost or paranormal activity from that location. This might involve performing an exorcism or cleansing or simply playing around with the energy in your house. You might need the help of either one of these people, and there are many out there to help. The problem is sifting through all the information to find the right fit for you.

There are professionals in the field who can help someone having a ghostly experience. The Society for Psychical Research (SPR, *www.spr.ac.uk/expcms*) was founded in 1882 and is based in London. This was the first organization established to investigate paranormal activity using scientific research. One of the society's aims has been to examine the question of whether we survive bodily death by evaluating the evidence provided by mediumship, apparitions of the dead, and reincarnation studies. The society's principal area of study includes the psychical research concerning exchanges between minds, or between minds and the environment, which are not dealt with by current orthodox science.

The American Society for Psychical Research (ASPR, *www.aspr.com*) is the oldest psychical research organization in the United States and is based in New York City. For more than a century, the ASPR has supported the scientific investigation of extraordinary or as-yet-unexplained phenomena that have been called psychic or paranormal. Over the years, investigators have found that upwards of 85 percent of all reported ghost sightings and hauntings have had other explanations. It's the unexplainable occurrences, however, that keep people fascinated with the paranormal.

Can a Ghost Hunter Help You?

These professionals are available, but the average person who thinks he has seen a ghost may be reluctant to call on professional help. How do you contact a professor at Duke University when your lights flicker every night at ten? Most people just want to understand what is happening, to have someone tell them they are not crazy and not alone. When someone believes he or she has seen, felt, heard, or somehow interacted with a ghost, is this simply a figment of an overactive imagination, an event that has happened sometime in the past that has somehow been imprinted at a location and is now being replayed, or is the witness actually seeing, hearing, feeling, smelling, or interacting with an intelligent entity that was once a living person?

Obviously, the paranormal experiences people have vary greatly. It's certainly possible that on rare occasions, when the situation is just right, people can communicate with entities. Maybe the experiences are a result of natural energy fields or energy anomalies that somehow act as a portal between the world of the living and those who have died. It is also possible that ghosts simply exist and roam freely among the living, but only those who decide to open their minds and believe are able to experience this phenomenon.

Believing that your own home is haunted or that you have seen the ghost of a departed relative or loved one can be a very traumatic and life-changing experience. If you are overwhelmed by the paranormal phenomena you have experienced, or you need or want to obtain a better understanding of what you are actually experiencing and why, consider seeking the assistance of a parapsychologist or paranormal investigator. When searching for guidance, however, make sure the people you turn to and decide to trust are credible and knowledgeable.

How to Find Help in Your Area

A simple search engine can start you on the path. No matter where you are, there are groups in your area willing to volunteer their skills. Finding one is easy, but finding one you can trust and who can actually help you is something very different. What should you look for in an investigator or group? The first thing should be the experience the group has. While newer groups can certainly be effective, people with more experience should have a wider frame of reference to help you. Be wary of groups whose Web sites consist solely of pictures of cemeteries. They might not have experience with homes, and their investigations might only consist of getting together on the weekend and finding haunted places. That is fine for advancing the field of ghost hunting, but it might not work for you. Look at their credentials. Many groups will offer services and not post their results. These groups can actually be trusted more. They help people but are not quick to place their clients in the limelight.

Never go with a group that charges you money. Most groups will ask for nothing, except maybe gas money, and the most expensive group is not necessarily the most knowledgeable. Above all, trust your gut; you are the best judge of what is right for you. Even though someone can say all the right things, investigators are people, and not all personalities click. You need people you can trust and who are going to work for you, not themselves. If an investigator makes you uncomfortable, either by his Web site or by your initial contact with him, cut off communication. You are not on the line for anything.

Having a haunting can be intimidating, and trying to get answers to what is going on can be just as stressful. Just know there are people out there who can help. You are not alone, and with the right support, you can find the help you need.

CHAPTER 3

PARANORMAL IN THE PRESENT

The landscape of paranormal investigation has changed dramatically in the past ten years, perhaps more than in any other decade in recent memory. But the goal remains the same—unlocking the eternal question of what happens after we die. What has changed, though, is the way people go about trying to prove it and how those explorers present that information to others. Ghost hunters have come a long way since the days of tipping tables, but the new ideas are usually just the old theories dressed up in modern clothes.

The Reconsideration of an Afterlife
For the past one hundred years or so, paranormal investigation has been in the hands of small, science-based societies devoted to proving or disproving paranormal activity. But before this, when the paranormal was directly linked to religious thought and speculation, the only promoters of the paranormal were the

mediums and the psychics. Most regular folks, while holding a belief ghosts might exist, did not take these people seriously. It was the time of the séance as a parlor game, and devices such as Ouija boards, pendulums, and dowsing rods were the main tools of the investigator.

A Look at Parapsychology

Parapsychology is the study of phenomena, real or supposed, that appear inexplicable under presently accepted scientific theories. The older term *psychical research* is still commonly used in Britain, but in America, the subject is generally called parapsychology. According to the Society for Psychical Research, in the early part of this century, the field of parapsychology was growing rapidly as more people were becoming interested in this field and were dedicating their professional lives to working in it. This has since changed, although the interest in the paranormal is still high, and people are straying away from the ideas of the parapsychologist.

The definition of parapsychology makes it difficult to set rigid limits on the topics included, but in practice, the focus of interest has been on the acquisition of information in unexplained ways such as extrasensory perception, or ESP, and on physical effects brought about in unexplained ways such as psychokinesis and paranormal healing.

The contemporary scene in psychical research involves work being done by philosophers, psychologists, and physicists, many of whom are on the faculty of distinguished universities and colleges both in the United States and abroad. Most parapsychologists and professional paranormal investigators take their work very seriously.

Increased Interest Sparked by *Ghost Hunters* the TV Show

The focus in the early days of paranormal investigation was communication. People went to a medium or attended a séance because they wanted to talk to people on the other side, mostly their relatives and loved ones. While groups such as the Society for Psychical Research were looking critically at the field, most still believed there was a veil between the average person and the ghostly realm. The existence of life after death was based on stories.

Paranormal investigation changed in October 2004 with the premiere of a new reality show, *Ghost Hunters*. The show revolved around a group of part-time paranormal investigators, the Atlantic Paranormal Society (TAPS), who went out in the field, gathered evidence, and presented it to the people who had asked them to come in. It also dealt with the difficulties in getting information, and in getting along with each other. The show was not only an immediate hit, but it changed the landscape of the paranormal field.

As ghosts became a hot topic, people began to go out more and to conduct their own investigations. Helped out by the Internet and new technology, people posted their findings and connected with people who shared their beliefs. Hitting the field with their own equipment, and inspired by TAPS, they explored the unknown in search of answers.

A True Ghost Expert

One of the most noted explorers of the unknown, Jeff Belanger, started his Web site Ghostvillage (*www.ghostvillage.com*) in 1999 when the field was much more sparse. His site continues to be the most popular ghost-related site on the Web, and he has seen the change in the field. Belanger says interest has increased, and this increase feeds itself, creating an atmosphere in which the average person is less intimidated to share her story or ask questions about things that have happened to her. Fewer people ask to have their names left off their experiences. Belanger has also seen a change in the types of things people want to talk about on his site. The first posts were about firsthand accounts, and while that section is still popular today, the sections on evidence have seen a steep incline, reflecting the influence of *Ghost Hunters* and TAPS' approach to looking at ghosts. It is less important to have experienced something and more important to have caught it on film.

New Equipment Empowers Investigators

Equipment has made the information of the unknown accessible to everyone. Not everyone is psychic, but anyone can use this technology to search for the answers. "All of a sudden, you're empowered," says Belanger. "You can take that equipment and get a glimpse of something. That's a big part of what draws more and more people in. People want magic, they want to know something is there, and this is one way to find out."

Ghost Hunters has solidified what ghosts are for many people and offered the blueprint for investigating. Ghost hunting groups, which had existed for years, began popping up all over the country with more frequency. There has also been a new level of organization within the groups, with jobs and titles clearly defined. Most groups have someone who specializes in EVPs and another who is an expert on the equipment the group uses. Groups have specialized members who may be authorities on cryptozoology, or the study of odd animals, and others who are the resident demonologists. At least two dozen groups also have an angelologist and a UFO specialist because they feel those fields are closely related to the study and investigation of ghosts.

The More Research the Better

Science is the focus of the paranormal field today, and many who have an interest in ghosts or who investigate the paranormal turn to science. They no longer want to just communicate. They want to prove, by a scientific method, that ghosts are real. In the past few years, that search has moved out of the lab and out of the hands of scientists and into the free time of people everywhere.

The science is based on a mix of theories and accepted beliefs held together by facts that show that the ideas seem to work. All science is fringe until it becomes established, but paranormal investigating seems to be looked down upon by everyone not interested in ghosts. Many investigators strive to have their ideas accepted by the scientific community, although their methods are not standardized, and their practice is based on flawed ideas.

Much of the science of investigating is based on what has worked in the past and what confirms the stories told by people who have had experiences. For example, cold spots have often been associated with paranormal activity. Someone sees a ghost and the room gets cold. The two become connected, so cold spots are proof that ghosts are present. An investigator then uses this idea to find phantoms by using equipment that measures temperature changes.

**Investigators Are Collecting
as Much as They Can**

Today's paranormal researchers hope to gather enough information to change people's minds. Their energy goes into collecting pictures with anomalies, recording voices on tape, and documenting odd energy in places that are thought to be haunted. At its best, some of this information confirms what has been said about a place. For example, a little girl has been seen in the staircase playing with a ball, and a picture is taken that shows a shadowy figure, a recording has an unknown voice of a little girl asking to play, the temperature drops at the time, and the electromagnetic readings of the room spike.

The trouble is these field investigators get little training and have no formal way to conduct their experiments or record their findings. The parapsychologists do not take what these investigators do seriously. The results of investigations are posted all over the Web and not in one place where they can be scrutinized by everyone.

Belanger feels centralizing the information out there is the most beneficial thing to the field of paranormal studies. The information gathered would be collected in the same way and forced to endure the same scrutiny. This collecting would create a database people could turn to evaluate trends and to begin critically looking at the science of what a ghost is. "Let's start to compile these things and see what we can find," says Belanger. And with this, it looks like the future might be to put the task back in the hands of the parapsychologist.

The Internet: A Database of Fact and Misinformation

The Internet has been both the best friend and the worst enemy of the paranormal community. The World Wide Web has allowed the sharing of information and evidence, but not all of the data is accurate. If used the right way, it can be a great resource, but cutting corners can lead you down the wrong path. Always consider something you read online as the starting point and not as truth.

There are so many resources online that a person can suffer a headache looking for the information he needs. Someone who has come into contact with a ghost no longer has to fear that he will be laughed at for coming forward, and the Internet becomes his voice. It has also raised the level of interest. Someone with a passing attraction can go online and feed her curiosity. This has created a wider base of information, and anyone can go and find local haunted areas to visit. The Internet offers so much more than just a good ghost story. It has given a new audience for ghost tours and authors with books to sell on the subject. All this publicity is a good thing at face value.

Some sites offer theories about ghosts or ideas that you might not have heard of before, but be wary of sources that contradict each other. Getting the information straight, especially when there is no centralized information bank, means sifting through many different sites and finding what is consistent. When viewing a site, think about the agenda of the people behind it. Are their beliefs in line with yours? The best-looking sites are not always the most accurate ones, so do not be tempted to believe the wrapping and not the content.

Take Advantage of the Information Out There
With so much information out there and public, a researcher can find out all he needs to know and never

had access to before. If a haunted house is related to a man who was murdered there or a suicide, a person can comb the archives of the local paper from the safety of his house without going into the town. He can get into local libraries, newspapers, town records, and information kept at historical commissions of towns. Even if an investigator cannot directly get the data, he can get the phone numbers, e-mail addresses, or mailing address of those who can do the research he needs. He can find out facts related to the case or even find out about hauntings with similar themes.

Surf with Caution

While the wealth of information out there has made researchers more educated, nothing replaces the details a researcher can get by stopping by the town hall or the local library. Visiting these places brings the researcher into contact with people who might know details firsthand or who may have information on another odd occurrence in the town as well as rumors floating around the town.

Finding the wrong information and stating it later as fact is also a problem facing researchers. People now can submit their experiences and list haunted places they know of without having to answer for what they have written.

Message boards are particularly susceptible to this. Many places that are listed online as being haunted do not exist or have their facts confused. Urban legends become cursed locations, and many Web masters, desperate for content, allow these stories to be passed on. Other sites just cut and paste the tales, and pretty soon one story, which may be filled with errors and untruths, can be on dozens of sites. There is also the phone-call element to the content on many sites. One person hears a story and retells it online. Someone else repeats it, and the details are slightly changed. This happens several times until the original story, which might have only been a rumor to begin with, is twisted and someone looking for a haunting in his area is given completely false information.

The Appeal of the False Haunting

People can be seduced by the evidence some sites offer. They have seen the television shows and want the most interesting and scary experiences. Genuine investigators have posted things they have found in different online forums, but so have people looking to make money or promote themselves. Interested parties can turn to search engines and find pages of evidence, but they can also find videos of ghosts or other unexplained occurrences. Sites like YouTube and MySpace post these videos with no one checking the credibility of the clips or the integrity of the investigators. This has allowed more evidence to proliferate and offers investigators the chance to learn how to investigate, but there are no disclaimers as to the truth of what is seen or expert analysis of what is on the screen. It is up to the viewer to use a critical eye.

Share and Gain Knowledge on a Message Board
Message boards play a major role in paranormal studies. Whether a board is connected to a paranormal Web site or even sponsored by a town, people can use it to get their ideas out there or collect information about the odd occurrences in their area. Boards are especially effective because they offer another level of anonymity to the poster. Usually one does not need to publish an e-mail address in a profile, meaning someone who truly does not want to be known can navigate these sites without anyone knowing who he is or how to contact him. This means someone can ask a question and sit back and watch people respond. For example, say someone asks, "Has anyone ever heard of a dark figure who appears walking in the park on Main Street late at night?" Someone who never would have shared her experiences might respond. Of course, this is a double-edged sword. With no chance of ever being held responsible, someone can post and spread information that is false.

Ghost Hunting Groups Online
One of the greatest things the Internet offers is the ability to bring people together who share similar interests. Nowhere is this more apparent than in the paranormal community, one of the fastest growing communities on the Net. Perhaps those who research the paranormal are more likely to be computer savvy and more likely to go online and find other groups. Perhaps they have been quiet too long, and as the audience for the

paranormal grows, there are more places to talk about experiences or investigations. People looking to connect with others who investigate can find someone who believes what they believe. Many sites are dedicated to setting up meetings between like-minded paranormal investigators. These sites often sponsor chat rooms and forums for people to connect or to share their thoughts and hunts. Like computer dating, one can register and find someone to go out with. Many of these sites do not charge, and you can find your paranormal soul mate while in the comfort of your house.

The Upside to Personal Web Sites

On the serious side, the Web has allowed people the opportunity to post what their groups do. With the ease of new HTML programs, anyone who investigates can write and publish a site quickly. This has led to a saturation of groups online from every state in the Union and many in other countries. For the investigator, having a Web address to publish findings means more credibility. In the past, casual investigators often gave up because they could not fund their research and received nothing from their hard work and time. Now ghost hunters can become celebrities, and their sites are their passages.

Most of the pages offer the same kind of content, making it hard to tell some groups apart. These should be used as entertainment or as references, but putting too much stock in local pages can cause you to shut yourself off to other paranormal possibilities. The foundation of these sites seems to be the local investigation, most often of local cemeteries. They offer intriguing evidence, such as orb photos and EVPs for download. This evidence often reinforces the stories about certain locations, and good sites will offer first-hand accounts of the investigated places to go along with the pictures.

It is a positive thing to have these sites out there, as the word about regional hauntings is what draws many people in. Most sites have a mission statement with details on the backgrounds of the people involved. One of the more interesting aspects of these pages is the number of different kinds of people working in the field. Some are blue-collar workers while others are professionals, proving that ghosts now seem to bring together all types of people. In some cases, this means families. There are more groups representing two or more generations. Hunting ghosts is now a family affair. Some groups have even started junior branches of their teams, offering teenagers the chance to learn how to investigate the paranormal while ensuring the next generation will keep up the interest.

A New Generation of Investigators

The better sites out there reflect the superior methods of the new generation of investigators. They offer ideas and theories about ghosts, but they also give advice on how to be responsible during an investigation and how to collect evidence in a safe way. Some have started organizations dedicated to saving historical areas or cleaning up cemeteries, while many get behind local and national charities and use their megaphones to raise money for organizations that need it.

One of the dangers is that an inexperienced group can follow the template it has seen online or on television and can get in the field and then post information without a real understanding of what it is doing. Some do not even need a full site to get their ideas out there. Blogs have made it possible to keep people informed about a group's activity without any knowledge of Web design and at no cost. Some newer groups find publishing their results on sites like MySpace allows them to spend more time out in the field than at home creating a site. They simply sign up, create a support network, and publish. This has allowed more people than ever to pursue their interest and allowed them to devote time to something that had no end result only a few years ago. Another of the negative turns has been a lack of ethics in getting the information out there, and the ease with which one can build a site has led to groups being split up.

The Paranormal Media

The paranormal has always been a way for people to connect. Since the days when people gathered around the fire to tell legends and myths, people have assembled to hear about the supernatural things going on around them. Whether it is a need to understand the universe or just to get together to see other people share the same questions and fears, ghosts bond people. As the means of communication have changed, the telling of ghost stories has evolved, as well. From the first written languages to the first mass-produced books and pamphlets, the paranormal has always been there, bringing people in, entertaining, and scaring generations. Early radio and television shows produced programs focused on the supernatural side of the universe and found them successful. Horror movies have always been popular, and every few years, there are cycles of theme-based offerings that make studios millions. In many ways, the media influence the way we think of paranormal ideas, but the media also give the people what they want.

How Things Have Changed in Recent Years

In recent years, the paranormal has given into the latest media trend, the replacement of dramatic, highly produced content with reality shows. In the 1980s and 1990s, shows such as *Unsolved Mysteries* and *In Search Of* offered viewers stories of real-life hauntings and the emotions of the people involved, but the new millennium has brought about a new type of show. People wanted to see real investigators out in the field looking for phantoms, and *Ghost Hunters* gave them what they were looking for. It not only changed everything for the people interested in finding ghosts, but it also encouraged other networks to find paranormal reality programs, many with a different or unique angle. One show might focus on a psychic, while another shows how a team might help local law enforcement. One show even had celebrities searching known haunted locations for ghosts. There have always been paranormal shows on television, but this marked a new era and a new way for viewers to get information on what a ghost might be and how to begin looking for one.

Local paranormal groups are now producing studio and location shows for their public-access stations. This is not a new idea. People have been creating neighborhood programming like this because of the cheap nature of it. Until recently, the shows were seen by a limited audience and maybe picked up by other nearby communities. The Internet has stepped in again. Now producers of these programs can post them on sites like MySpace and YouTube, and the shows can be seen by a larger audience. This allows self-produced series to reach a wider audience than ever before and feeds the public's need for ghosts stories and information on the supernatural.

Radio Buzzes with Ghost Talk

Radio has seen a surge in paranormal programming, as well. Local stations, especially on the AM dial, where there is more talk radio, have had their share of ghost shows, but they were much more focused on local hauntings and telling a good story. People listened in, but more because it was the equivalent of sitting around a campfire getting themselves scared. There are the heavy hitters who have been doing it for years and keeping the talk alive. Coast to Coast AM and Dreamland were created and originally hosted by Art

Bell and set the bar for shows that followed. The tradition continues with George Noory, who now hosts Coast to Coast AM, and Whitley Streiber, who is the host of Dreamland.

The new trend, however, focuses more on investigations and investigators and getting information out there. Instead of the stories being the driving force, people are looking for the ideas.

Local Radio Shows Get a Good Following

Tim Weisberg is a sports reporter from southeastern Massachusetts who also hosts *Spooky Southcoast*, a local radio show that has made the transition from a local audience to a national and sometimes international base of listeners. Technology, such as podcasts and live Internet streaming, has drawn in a larger group of people to the show. Weisberg reports that AM radio stations, which are struggling to keep younger audiences, are now more willing to give people a chance to start shows like *Spooky Southcoast*, especially after seeing the success of similar online shows. The increase in audience mirrors what other stations are experiencing, and their approach has proven crucial to getting people to tune in. Weisberg believes that the main audience will always be those into the paranormal looking for as many voices and opinions as possible, but he notices more and more listeners outside that circle responding to the show. Whenever he has psychics on the show, the call boards light up. On those nights, the callers are local residents with something to offer.

The Appeal of Ghost Radio

Part of the show's success and part of the success of shows like it are live remotes or programs done from haunted places. People cannot make it out to many of these locations themselves, and to hear a show from someplace like Gettysburg or the *Queen Mary* automatically transports them there. Regardless of whether anything happens during the show, listeners feel as if they have been to these famous places. *Spooky Southcoast* has made a habit of utilizing these types of remote broadcasts. For example, on a show about the famously haunted Bridgewater Triangle in Massachusetts, they had several groups at ghostly hot spots while authorities in the studio commented and told the background of the places. This programming draws people in because they can find out about the places around them from the safety of their homes.

Radio shows have to strike a balance between presenting information and keeping people interested in a new world in which information can be gathered at the speed of light. It is difficult to produce a show about something many people believe does not exist, but the larger issue is giving a voice to people whose opinions are often very different. The trick, and what the best shows do well, is to offer as many different guests and as many different ideas as possible. This kind of approach makes for good debate, but it also offers an outlet for differing views.

The Best of the Best

Haunted America Tours (*www.hauntedamericatours*
.com) is a popular Web site that offers guests a way to
find the best haunted tours in their areas. The site also
has expanded to offer interviews with experienced
ghost hunters and poll questions that look to measure
people's ideas about ghosts. In the summer of 2007, the
site producers asked people to name the best paranormal radio shows on the air. This is what people said:

1. *Coast to Coast AM*
   www.coasttocoastam.com
2. *Psi Talk Radio Webcast*
   www.psitalk.com
3. *Ghostly Talk*
   www.ghostlytalk.com
4. *Alabama ParaSpiritual Research Radio*
   www.apsrradio.com
5. *Parahub Radio*
   www.parahub.org
6. *The Hilly Rose Show*
   www.fatemag.com/radio
7. *Darkness on the Edge of Town*
   www.darknessradio.com
8. *Shadow Talk Paranormal Radio*
   www.shadowtalkparanormalradio.com
9. *The Lou Gentile Show*
   www.lougentile.com
10. *TAPS Para-Radio*
    www.tapspararadio.libsyn.com

Web-Based Radio Shows

Then the field evolved again. As the Internet continues to grow, people are finding it easier to get the word out. Now paranormal groups host their own paranormal radio shows that exist only as Web-based programs. A group can produce a show from home and broadcast it live over a host channel on the Internet. A simple Internet search will reveal shows in most communities across the country. These shows focus on the activities of the groups making them and also the local paranormal scene. People can find out about the areas where they live, and since most shows are archived for weeks or months, people can listen when it is most convenient for them. There is no need to tune in at a certain time to a certain station.

The offerings online are a mixed bag. "One thing I've noticed, because of the boom in Internet radio, it's become so easy to have a radio show," says Weisberg. There is a danger in having hosts who spread the wrong information to serve their agendas or only use the airwaves to promote themselves and their friends. There is also a danger of having too much of a good thing. "I used to believe that was going to saturate the market and lessen the impact of what we say," Weisberg adds. "I've come around now. It's just more voices and angles, and that can't hurt."

Ghosts in Print

The printed word has seen a surge in paranormal material, as well. Book publishers have seen an increase in the need for books about ghosts, especially in regional stories. The more intriguing aspect of this is the rise of additional paranormal magazines. While publications like *FATE* and *Skeptical Inquirer* have been popular for years, smaller, ghost-focused magazines have hit the shelves of major bookstores across the nation. TAPS promotes several titles. Publications like *Ghost!*, *Mysteries*, and *Haunted Times* fill this new need. There also are online magazines about paranormal subjects. The Internet allows publishers to make a good product without having to pay the overhead costs of printing and distribution. When you throw in online newsletters from ghost Web sites and investigators, there is no end to the amount of time you can devote to reading about apparitions.

PART 2

CHILLING TRUE STORIES COME TO LIFE

Before there were television shows or EMF readings, before there was even the term ghost hunter, there were the stories. True accounts of the paranormal draw us in because we identify with the characters. We see ourselves as the ordinary people caught up in the drama. Ghost stories are the foundation of our knowledge of the other side. We can take all of the readings we want and record all of the EVPs we need, but the tales are what we heard first. The heart of the haunting, the people touching what cannot always be seen and experiencing what we fear and are attracted to, is what really makes the dark a little unnerving.

These stories are all true, or at least told as true, and the people who lived through them shared what had happened to them for different reasons. Some wanted the word to get out; for many, it is enough to know that they are not alone in being the victims of hauntings. Whenever possible and where the people have agreed, real names have been used.

Many first shared their experiences on Archive X (*www.wirenot.net/X*), Obiwan's UFO-Free Paranormal Page (*www.ghosts.org*), or Massachusetts Paranormal Crossroads (*www.masscrossroads.com*), while many got in touch with me directly. All agreed to have their stories in this book and share a snapshot of their lives.

CHAPTER 4

THE OUIJA BOARD MIXED BAG

Throughout history, people have made incredible claims as to the power of their Ouija boards. For example, according to the Museum of Talking Boards, in the late 1900s, Mrs. John Howard Curran channeled an entity she called Patience Worth, and through the Ouija board produced six novels, hundreds of pages of poetry, and a selection of other literary works. It was believed to be Worth who actually wrote the novels but Curran who channeled the information. Another author, named Emily G. Hutchings, was reported to have contacted the spirit of Mark Twain when she wrote a novel called *Jap Heron*. In more modern times, Iris Maloney is reported to have won $1.4 million in the California State Lottery after picking her numbers using her Ouija board.

Not all the stories are that dramatic. Most people who use Ouija boards get little more than mumbled messages that they cannot understand. Trying to communicate in this way is not unique, but the effect is cumulative. The more someone uses the board, the more intense the experiences become, and not all of them are positive.

Talking to the Cheerleader

FLINT, MICHIGAN

In Michigan, football is big business. The South may have the right to claim the most rabid high-school football fans, but Michigan is not far behind. The players take on the status of mythic heroes, and the cheerleaders hold a place above the regular crowd. They can become the subjects of myths, too.

People on the other side want to talk. Whether they're trying to make some sense out of what has happened to them, to share a part of their lives, or to try and enter the user's life for a more sinister reason, ghosts need some kind of company. People you knew in life can find you too, even if you were never friends. Chris knew of the popular cheerleader who had gone to the same high school he did, but she didn't talk to him until after she had passed.

Chris was never really close to Kelly. He actually only knew her in passing and would never have spoken to her. She was the head cheerleader and three years older than he was. She was friendly and involved in everything, so it was not unusually hard to find her if she was in the room. When she graduated from high school she came back and became the assistant cheer-leading coach, and he would see her in the gym during practice or on the campus talking to old teachers. She was, from afar, someone who enjoyed life and gave back to the community she had gotten so much from.

When Chris went to college, he began using a Ouija board on a regular basis. When he and his group of friends played, they created their own rituals. One night, they set up their candles and played their usual music and prepared to talk to whoever decided to stop in. "Things were going pretty well. We had spoken to a few weak spirits, asking questions about how they had died and making jokes when we got weird answers. I was asked by a spirit to be given permission to come into the room. There are some rules against this, but we didn't take the bad things we heard seriously. I agreed, joking I hoped it was a pretty girl. When I did, it said it knew me from high school. I asked her name, and the spirit asked me to open up my fresh-man yearbook to page 17. It was the seniors."

Chris asked if the spirit was anyone he knew. The planchette moved to "yes." The pointer then spelled out Kelly's name, and she was the fourth picture in the first row on the page. "I thought maybe it was a spirit just looking over my shoulder picking out a name at random until I got back together with an old girlfriend. She had been a cheerleader, and once she asked me if I knew whether her old cheerleading coach, Kelly, had died in a car accident."

Guarding the House

DALLAS, TEXAS

Boards sometimes have the ability to see what we cannot. Critics have a hard time explaining this because it goes against the idea of the user's unintentionally moving to get the answers he wants. People have been known to consult a Ouija board when they need advice, and they find the answers, whether they come from somewhere outside of our world or not, to be useful. It is unknown whether spirits have some sense of the future, as if time does not exist for them and so they do not predict as much as they merely tell what they see. Others believe ghosts look above a scene, able to see who they are talking to but also the whole world laid out before them. It is also said they can read the hearts and minds of the living, a kind of ghostly sixth sense. If a spirit has enough vision, it may be better than having your own private security guard.

When Jenna would walk to Nicole's house, she would have to take the shortcut that led her across the street from presidential hopeful Ross Perot's mansion in Dallas. One night, some friends of hers had too much to drink, and they stumbled onto the front lawn, only to be escorted by several of the rifle-toting guards who roamed the grounds. Their protection did not extend all the way to Nicole's house, but one night the friends had the next-best thing.

Jenna was staying at Nicole's house while Nicole's parents were away. The house was haunted, and they had experienced several hauntings there over the years, especially when they were alone. One night, they decided to have some friends sleep over. They invited Nicole's cousin Mallori, who had lived in a haunted house most of her life and had spent time developing her psychic abilities. She kept in contact with several spirits, including her spirit guide. As soon as she entered the house, she was uncomfortable. She suggested that they all use the Ouija board to try to make contact with the ghosts she felt were in the house.

They set it up near the sliding glass door, and Jenna noticed a figure standing in the entryway twenty feet away. It was small and outlined in a green glowing light. Someone else saw it, too, but in a different color. They tried several times to re-create the glow by turning lights on and off and moving people around the room. The only way the figure would return was when they all put their hands back on the board.

"We started using the board again and got an eighteen-year-old girl named Nina who had died in a car accident. She was disoriented and scared, and this was causing the weird things in the house. As she talked, the glowing figure came back again and would change color. It would fade in and out and get brighter the more frustrated she'd get. It was kind of sad. I felt like I was feeling her emotions as my own," remembers Jenna.

The movements of the planchette started to change as it moved across the board. It began making circles and moving much faster. "She started to spell out 15, 16, 15. Guns, boys, 15, 16," Jenna says. Mallori was nervous and sent her boyfriend and his friend out to check the yard. After a few seconds, they heard him scream back, 'Hey, get the hell out of here.' When he came back in, he told us there had been two kids, about sixteen years old, walking around in the woods outside the house with a gun, trying to break in."

Mallori eventually helped Nina cross over to the other side, and as she did, Jenna saw the figure fade away. They never heard from her again, and after that, the noises in Nicole's house stopped.

The Obsession

DANVILLE, VIRGINIA

Most people who use a board never have a problem. The younger the user, the more defenseless and willing the victim, the more quickly a simple toy can become a nightmare. There are a select few who seem to have had a board take over their world, and most who fall prey have some other underlying problem, something that draws in the darker spirits. Sometimes it is an addiction or a mental health disorder, but more often than not the emptiness that draws the person to a Ouija board is the same that brings the bad spirits and demons, smelling blood like sharks.

Jay is not a typical teenager, although her story is not unusual. She lives in a small town on the border of Virginia and North Carolina, just where the South starts to be the South. The town is not known for its hauntings, although there are a few that attract ghost hunters to the area. But there is a strong gothic underground there, born out of monotony and uneasiness with local traditions. In a place like Virginia, the occult becomes a strong form of teen rebellion. Jay experimented with the supernatural but enjoyed the distance between the fantasy of the dark and the reality some fall into.

There was not much to do in Jay's small town. Playing with a Ouija board became a way to break up the day, a way to make the stories of vampires and werewolves seem more real and still be safe. She was like many who abuse a board, and she displayed all the warning signs people in that situation do. They plan their days around using Ouija boards, often asking questions and using them by themselves. Any obsession is dangerous, but when a darker element is waiting in the wings, compulsive use of a Ouija board may be the sign of a demonic attack. What starts out innocently soon spirals out of control, and only when the user stops depending on the communication can she break free and avert danger. Sometimes the board has a way of coming back.

Jay discovered the Ouija board like many people do. A friend began using it, and Jay, only mildly interested at first, began to play along. One of the common misconceptions of the board is that you need to buy a classic model to make contact with the spirit world.

Any materials can be used to construct one, even a piece of paper and a guitar pick. When her friends stopped using it, she made one of her own, curious if it would work.

"At first, it was fun," she says. "I contacted people, and they came and went, but then I slowly became absorbed. Not really slowly. It was actually fairly quick. I destroyed a few, but I always made more. Soon it became that even at school I would make one on the paper under my work. It was as if I couldn't stop."

Aside from taking up more and more of her time, the communications began to get eerie, scaring her but not making her give up the new addiction. "There was this one guy that kept saying he loved me. He said he had committed suicide in his teens. He kept saying that I was his 'baby' and wanted to have sex with me."

She continued to make boards out of anything she could find, destroying them and making more. The spirit world was about to come off the board for her. "I knew I was becoming possessed by it when I didn't have to use a board anymore to talk to them. I naturally have a lot of spiritual energy and am sensitive to paranormal activity. I'm not sure how I talked to them, but it was like I could hear the letter before they moved the dial to that letter. It was like that in my head. They were never silent. They would say anything to get me to talk to them. I think that what they want is energy, and since I had an abundance of it, they stayed around me."

A trained professional would have seen the demons circling Jay's life. Possession was close. She only knew her life was falling apart. "My room stopped being a safe place for me. I couldn't get dressed because I could feel eyes watching me. I have a large mirror over my dresser, and I just knew that they watched me from it somehow."

While demons, like angels, are sexless, there seems to be a certain attraction to females from the demonic realm, and their obsession and possession take the form of seduction and sexual advances. Perhaps they just know the best way to get to their victim, because the peeping Tom spirit was rattling Jay and making her feel unsafe and constantly under attack.

The most mundane activity ended up saving her life. "It was around this time that I cleared my room out so that I could paint it. I slept in my sister's room next door and covered the mirror with a large blanket. My room calmed down, I think, because it lacked energy without me in it. Over time, I ignored the voices, and they faded. I kept telling them that I didn't want them there, performed several incantations to close the door to unwanted spirits, and mentally shut the psychic door to them. I think this helped."

Although everything returned to normal for Jay, she now sees how close she came to losing complete control. "Over time, they faded away, and now I don't hear them. I don't dare make another wretched board, and I advise against it."

Jay is still active in the underground gothic scene in her area, and she still has a strong interest in ghosts and the paranormal. Now she prefers to observe the paranormal from the outside.

The Unusual Tale of Federal Government

BOSTON, MASSACHUSETTS

There are certain elements that have to be in place to have a great ghost story. It should take place in a haunted locale, and the main characters should be stupid kids who step out of their innocent world and get caught in the storm. Their lives should be in danger from an unseen force, maybe something evil that has an agenda. There should be a twist at the end, such as finding out that the ghost has been seen before by others who nearly escaped its grip themselves. You need a good setting, and what better setting than a college dormitory in Boston, home to more universities than any other city in America. The city becomes more important when you consider that the characters are Emerson students, living in the old Charlesgate Hotel in Boston. It was considered one of the most haunted buildings in Massachusetts, and the college had made a rule that no student could use any type of spirit communication, especially a Ouija board, in the dorm.

The story of Federal Government is a true ghost story. It is unclear what kind of spirit he was, but he seemed to be a powerful spirit with negative intentions, a long memory, and some influence on our world.

For a week in the spring of 1995, a group of college friends spent too much time using a board. They were not only breaking the rules of trying to talk to the dead, but they were also breaking the rules of their college. They had gotten mixed results all week, engaging them and keeping them on for hours but not saying anything they could verify. Nothing scared them, and one spirit came often, saying it was one of their guardian angels. It was looking after them all and warning of a dark soul nearby. The group was familiar with this kind of talk. Most ghosts would say anything to make the users stay on.

One night, a very strong spirit pushed a weaker one off. Tim was almost immediately intimidated. "He immediately told us to be scared. When we asked what we should have been scared of, the pointer moved slowly over the OUIJA label on the top of the board, slowly enough to give me goose bumps."

The friends were a bit frightened by the experience and quit for the night, but the next night they were back on. Almost immediately, the spirit came on again. Every time they tried to talk, the ghost would push off anyone else and make itself known. It said its name was Federal Government, which seemed like an odd name for a spirit. But it knew everything about them. It could spell out their family members and their birthdays, and it had a sense of humor, making fun of them and other people in the dormitory.

"Federal Government became obsessed with one of my roommates at the time," Tim remembers. "He would refuse to talk while he was in the room or say nasty things about him. Mike was a womanizer and I had joked earlier that semester that he was sleeping his way through the alphabet. We asked Federal Government why he did not like Mike, and he said because he made girls cry. When we asked how he made girls cry, it scrolled through all the letters on the board in a Z motion."

The scroll became the ghost's signal that it wanted to talk. It refused to let any other spirits on the board and only wanted to talk about Mike. It said he had to die, and it was its goal to make sure that happened. The friends tried to laugh it off at first, telling the phantom it had no power in their world. Once when they challenged it, it caused the fire alarm to go off.

"It wasn't until he almost killed Mike [that] we took its threats seriously and understood the kind of power it had. We were using the board and Mike went to take a shower. We were talking to a spirit that claimed it was one of our guardian angels, and Federal Government came on. It spelled out 'HAHAHAHA.' When we asked why it was laughing, it spelled out 'ACDCACD-CACDC.' We were all confused until Mike came back into the room. His hair was wet, and the color was gone from his face."

It seemed that Federal Government had found its chance to get at his victim. When Mike had gone to use the shower, the light had been out. He screwed it back in and began the shower. Just as he was washing his hair, the light went out. His first instinct was to screw the light in again, but he stopped. He was soaking wet and standing in a pool of water. He washed his hair in the dark rather than risking electrocution.

Ouija board stories are often tales of coincidence. People living them see all the signs, but things can be explained away by outsiders. Federal Government was not through touching the college students. Serena was an old girlfriend of Mike's. They had dated on and off over the years, and their relationship almost always ended with Mike doing something horrible to her. They talked that summer, and he brought up ghosts. Serena said she believed in them because she had talked to someone who claimed to be the Devil. She had first talked to him when she was young, and he had told her that when she died he would have her. Her soul was his forever, and he was just waiting for her to die so he could claim his prize. When she had used the board earlier that year, the same spirit had gotten on, asking her if she remembered him. She said she knew he was not the Devil and begged for his real name. The spirit said his name was Federal Government.

The Haunted Hotel

Just down the subway line from Charlesgate is one of the most famously haunted buildings in Boston. Known as one of the higher-end hotels in the city, the Omni Parker House Hotel is as known for the ghosts that walk from room to room as it is for the famous people who have stayed there over the years, such as Ho Chi Minh, who worked in the dining room, and John Wilkes Booth, who stayed there before heading out to Ford's Theatre. The hotel, recently renovated and expanded, is like a museum of the history of Boston, and when people share the stories of Bill Clinton's stay there, they always end by talking about the ghost who lives there, too.

The upper floors have been the scenes of many odd balls of light and unexplained noises. Some people have seen full-bodied apparitions walking the halls and appearing in rooms, sometimes waking up guests. The elevator has been known to start running by itself and to stop on the third floor. There is never any harm done to patrons, but that does not stop them from wanting to leave.

The most-written-about room is 303. A man is said to have killed himself there in the 1940s, and the room was the scene of so much activity that the management was forced to convert it to storage. There have been loud knocking sounds, fires, and unexplained odors of cigar smoke and whiskey.

CHAPTER 5

HAUNTINGS IN THE NORTHEAST

New England ghost stories are some of the oldest and richest in the United States; they've been reworked over cold winters and hundreds of years. From the writings of the first settlers of the country to the Salem witch trials to the modern day Bridgewater and Bennington Triangles and the cemeteries of Connecticut, New England can trace its history through the ghosts its people have seen. The stories get even deeper as you move south and west toward the dark fields of Pennsylvania, the heart of popular paranormal researcher Hans Holzer's work. Many of the ghost stories in the area rely on an old standby to explain when something goes wrong: ancient Native American burial grounds. While there are many hauntings that stem from our indiscretions and use of older lands, stories like the ones included here do not need any help.

The Lady in White

GOFFSTOWN, NEW HAMPSHIRE

Goffstown should be off the country's map. It is a small rural town outside of Manchester, New Hampshire, with a population so small the local high school services several towns in the area. Goffstown, however, is anything but quiet. It came into the national spotlight in the late 1980s and early 1990s when a rash of suicides invited the media to dub it "Suicide USA." Goffstown suffered an increased rate of teenage emotional trouble, drug use, and cult activity. It also became known as a haunted town, with many of the hauntings having no explanation.

Linda and Leo lived in their home for eighteen years, and if you had asked them if they had ever seen a ghost, they would have laughed at you. It would have been a lie. From the outside, the house was an ideal place to raise their three children, but its isolated location also gave it a sense of dread. It seemed the ideal sight for something supernatural to happen, but it was not until the death of a close family member that they were visited by a mysterious and comforting presence, one they still cannot explain today and one that they avoided talking about, like the secrets of a small town.

Shortly after the death of Leo's aunt, Linda was lying on the couch in the den when she felt someone in the room with her. After a few seconds, she looked up to see a young woman dressed in white standing at the doorway, looking up with a blank expression. "She looked like she was lost and she didn't realize what was going on," Linda recalls. After a few minutes, the woman moved backwards and dissolved into the darkness.

Linda describes the woman as all in white, wearing a nightgown of see-through linen. She was in her thirties and of average height, with long, curly red hair that came out the bottom of a scarf or something else on her head. Linda remembers most the expression on her face, "like she was just passing through," and the fact that she could see through her. The sighting was easily ignored. It had been late, and she had had a tough day at work. Perhaps she had just imagined it. Nothing had ever happened before that, and despite the death of her husband's aunt, there had been no tragedies to invite anything in. Besides, Linda was a logical person, and to her, ghosts did not exist.

She now questions that belief. Over the next year and a half, Linda saw the woman about ten more times, always at night, always at the doorway of her den. "I would stare at her. I would try to figure out what she was doing there, and then she'd be gone." She says there was nothing that would preface the woman's arrival, and it happened during any season. She would just appear. The woman never tried to talk to her. In fact, Linda says the woman never seemed to see her there and never tried to interact in any way. She does say that the appearance of the ghost was comforting and soothing.

"There was just something about her. Maybe it was her face. She never smiled, but she was warm. I think she was looking after me too," Linda says. Once, when her husband was in trouble while taking a trip in West Africa, she had sensed that something was wrong. "I felt she was my guardian angel in a way. I sent her to help him." When he arrived home safely, that he said he had felt something at the moment things were at their worst, as if there had been someone with him all of a sudden. Even when witnesses can't make sense of them, ghosts often are the doorway to other unexplained things.

When Leo was safe at home, the hauntings continued, and the silence remained. Other things were happening, but he and Linda refused to believe that they were connected. Their new dogs, eager to jump and run throughout the house, refused to enter the den. Then there was the mysterious stain on their ceiling that remained even though they painted over it several times, bleached it, and investigated to find no pipes or trails of water leading to it. It meant nothing by itself, but the new ghost was making herself known to Linda's husband, as well. Leo, who spent his professional career as a private investigator and security officer, relies on facts. If Linda is logical, Leo is rational and cynical. He still has trouble explaining away his experiences with the woman in white. He saw her several times, at the foot of his bed and in the den, and his description of the woman mirrors his wife's. "She never looked at me but stared straight ahead, with a blank expression. Each time she would be there and then be gone in a few seconds. It doesn't have any reason to it, and I don't like to talk about it," he says.

Neither Leo nor Linda mentioned the ghost until they moved to Nashua, New Hampshire, two years after the appearances started. The house had become too big for the family. Their youngest child had moved out before the mysterious woman revealed herself, and both Leo and Linda thought the other would think they were out of their mind. Although their leaving had nothing to do with the pale figure, they still wonder what became of her.

They are not sure why she was there to begin with. She appeared shortly after their son had left the house, and a year later, they were gone. Looking back, Linda wonders if she was there to help them transition somehow. She still thinks that the house felt less empty on the nights the woman visited.

In the paranormal world, this is known as a residual haunting. The ghost may be some sort of energy left behind and replayed. Residual hauntings tend to remain in the places where the energy was released. The spirit seems to have something to do with the site; she's somehow connected to or trapped in the dwelling. Evidence suggests that it might be the family that drew the ghost, because there is no negative history to the house. The woman in white was clearly Caucasian, dispelling any theory that the woman was a Native American who might have lived on the land. When the family moved in, the house was only two years old, and no tragedy had ever happened there. The first owners had moved out shortly after moving in, but Linda claims it was not under unusual circumstances.

Before that, the land was undeveloped and owned by a local Catholic school. The school had a convent that housed several dozen nuns, although over the years, their numbers were reduced.

Linda feels this explains the woman, but is quick to dismiss the headpiece as a habit or the woman, although comforting, as particularly religious. This explanation, even in an unexplainable situation, makes the most sense. "Who else could it be?" Linda says.

Despite the long tenure of the family, the house has not had a good life since their departure. At least four other families have lived in the house in the ten years since Leo and Linda moved out. All have suffered financial and personal headaches before leaving.

The Night I Met Mary Gately

DEDHAM, MASSACHUSETTS

We often do not realize that the moments that will change our lives are upon us until they are in the rearview mirror. We see their importance only after they have passed and we think of all the things we could have done differently. People who experience the paranormal often come face to face with the most significant experiences of their lives, and before they can process them, they're over. They then have a life-time to speculate, wondering what brought them to the park that night or what attracted them to the house they now cringe to enter. Kenny, a former resident of

East Dedham, Massachusetts, met the woman who would change his ideas about life almost thirty years ago—unfortunately, she was dead.

On October 27, 1977, Kenny experienced something that would have a profound effect on his life, so profound that he recites the date from his teenage years today without even thinking about it. He was walking to his grandparents' house in East Dedham at about 4:30 P.M., just as the sun was setting. Unlike other teenagers, he enjoyed spending time with his grandparents and often made the short trip from his house.

As he walked, he noticed an odd, sparkling glow underneath a streetlight about 150 yards away. Since it was Halloween time, he thought it might be a Halloween decoration, but as he got closer, he saw it was the perfect image of a woman. Thinking it might be a gag, he kept walking toward her, looking for some type of projector creating the image, but the closer he got the more defined her face and features became. As he got several yards from the image, he realized he was staring at a ghost.

"The woman was in her late thirties or early forties, tall, with her hair tied up in a bun and pinned down," Kenny recalled. "She was wearing a long, pleated dress almost to the ground with puffy shoulders, but her feet were clearly several inches above the pavement. One odd feature I still remember is her long fingernails. The entire figure was in white, and she seemed translucent, as if she were a projection. I looked around for something that was throwing her up there. She was completely still. She stood with her mouth open and her hands out and her palms up. She was not in this world, but I could see every line of her face and every wrinkle of her clothes."

He became convinced that he was seeing a ghost when he began to circle the woman. He was three or four feet from her, and she appeared in three dimensions, hologram technology too advanced for the late seventies. "I wasn't scared," he says. "More like curious. I thought there might be a reason she was there."

During the encounter, the street was silent, and he felt that there should have been more activity or that someone would come by and see them. He asked her name and if there was any reason for her to appear, but she did not move or speak.

His mind went straight to his elderly grandparents. Ghosts are often harbingers of something else significant about to happen, especially the passing of someone close to the viewer's life. "I thought there might be something wrong with my grandparents and ran to their house."

Kenny arrived winded and a bit nervous. They asked him what was wrong, but he stayed silent until his grandfather asked him why he was off. Kenny eventually opened up and told him the whole story, but his grandfather did not seem startled by his tale. He had experienced something similar when he was younger in that same area while he was working a pony cart. It was just dark when he saw a woman come out of the woods, and he knew it was a ghost. He whipped the horse to get out of there quickly and never went on the road after that when it was dark.

His grandfather attributed it to a story he had heard about a man who either had killed his wife and dumped her in the water to be found later or had killed her near the water. The brook where she was found became known as Murder Brook. Kenny's grandfather believed that he had seen the murdered woman walking from the water to her house, trying to get home.

Although his grandfather was known as being a bit off center, Kenny believed him. He held his feeling inside, though, never daring to tell anyone for fear of being thought crazy or ridiculed. It was not until he was pressed because of his change of mood that he finally told his closest friend, Tom. Tom was silent about the haunting but came back a while later and said he wanted Kenny to meet someone.

Kim was slightly younger than the boys, but she had told Tom a story and had sworn him to secrecy. Murder Brook ran through her backyard, and for the past ten years, she had seen the ghost of a woman at the foot of her bed. "She said it would happen two or three times a year and disturbed her greatly," Kenny says. "We compared notes and realized it was the same woman down to the last detail."

Research shows that there was a murder like the one Kenny's grandfather described. Although there is no body of water known as Murder Brook, and the Dedham Public Library and the Dedham Historical

Society were unable to find any reference to it in any literature, there is a Mother Brook nearby. But it is not connected to the crime.

In 1881, James Gately killed his wife by beating her with an ax handle. The real reason for her murder remains a mystery, but Gately was quoted as saying he hit her to pacify her. He then walked to a brook nearby, washed his bloodied self off, and went back to the house to go back to sleep in his son's room. Although the autopsy report states that she died of one fatal blow to the head, the room was covered in blood and struck police at the time as the worst murder they had ever seen. He was brought to trial a year later and found not guilty by reason of insanity.

Crime or no crime, the woman remains with Kenny today. "It made me rethink what I believe. Nothing I knew before that could explain her."

The Red-Headed Hitchhiker of Route 44

REHOBOTH, MASSACHUSETTS

The world has a long tradition of haunted roads, and in America, most states boast stories of phantoms seen by people in cars. Many of the stories are mere folklore, and the ghost hitchhiker is one of the most popular and frightening urban legends. For every legend out there, a true ghost, witnessed by locals, makes itself known. Most of these cases borrow from the classic myths.

New England has its own version of the story. In some versions, the ghost is a scary but sympathetic figure, but the Red-Headed Hitchhiker of Route 44 is the exact opposite. A large man with red hair and a thick red beard, dressed in a flannel red shirt, is the terror of one of the most haunted areas of southern Massachusetts. His eyes are always described as giving him away. They have been described as vacant or empty, and at times, they have been said to glow red or yellow.

Although he has never physically attacked anyone, his intent is to scare, and few who have come across him are sympathetic to his plight. He has been known to appear in people's cars and scare them or to take control of a car, making himself known over the radio or causing the automobile to stall. Many have seen him on this dark and lonely highway, hitchhiking or resting on the side of the road. Witnesses have looked out their windows to see him staring at them, even as their cars travel at high speeds. As with many roadside apparitions, drivers sometimes hit him when he is in the middle of the road. When they stop, there is no evidence of hitting anything and no sign of the red-haired man. They do hear him laughing and taunting them. On rare occasions, he has forced cars to stall and then appeared in their headlights when they stop, staring at them before dissolving.

Over the years, many people have spotted the ghost, but more have heard stories from their friends about other people who have spotted the phantom. Much of the lore of the Red-Headed Hitchhiker has fallen into the realm of urban legend. One new tale is that if you drive to the town line and honk your horn three times, he will appear in your headlights. They also say that if you are driving with three people in the car near the town line, he will appear in the empty seat. To some, this means he does not exist, but do not be fooled. The original reports were told by reliable witnesses, and more genuine reports come in if a researcher is patient and sifts through the legends. The people in Rehoboth know him to be real, and they drive with their knuckles a bit whiter at night.

The Haunted Triangle

If you are trying to plan a paranormal vacation, there might be no better place than a section of southeastern Massachusetts known as the Bridgewater Triangle. Formed by the towns of Abington, Freetown, and Rehoboth, Massachusetts, the area offers everything a seeker of the supernatural is looking for. It has long been known as a hot spot for odd animals, including Bigfoot, extremely large birds, Mothman, and evil dogs who roam the evil swamp near the dog track. The triangle has been the playground of UFOs and men in black.

The area is also known as one of the most haunted tracts of land in New England. In addition to the Red-Headed Hitchhiker, visitors can track the Mad Trucker of Copicut Road in Freetown, enroll at Bridgewater State College and search several haunted dorms, and roam any of the dozen haunted cemeteries in Taunton. The sheer number of abandoned asylums is worth the trip. Stop a resident, and you will find that you are a stone's throw away from a haunting. Of course, if you want to spend more than a day, you can stay at the Lizzie Borden Bed and Breakfast, where the ghost of the acquitted murderer is said to haunt the room.

Just Passing Through

HIGHLAND, NEW YORK

Most people find experiences with the paranormal to be profound, if unexplained, events in their lives. They are somehow different afterward. People see their dead relatives or gain some insight into something they were having trouble with. There are reports of a family member intervening when someone was on the brink of suicide. Sometimes, however, touching the other side is too brief or too mundane to bring any revelation. The witness gets a glimpse of the other side only to have it be as normal as her daily life. Maybe it is this feature that makes it so unsettling.

Deirdre and her husband moved into their house in Highland, New York, in 2000, after falling in love with the old house. She says that when they first saw the house, and even after moving into it, she never felt it gave off an eerie, ghostly feeling, and friends never commented on anything strange. Almost from the start, however, she knew something was not right.

"The second time we spent the night here, we each had very similar dreams. We dreamt about three boys playing with guns, and one was accidentally shot dead. A few weeks later, we had learned that our home was almost two hundred years old and used to be a boys school back in the 1930s. It turns out that back then a group of young boys got into the old barn next door, finding rifles and taking a couple of them. They were playing around with them, but unfortunately there was an accident. One boy lost his life. He was shot."

Although the dreams had been bizarre, they did not think about them too much. It was a coincidence with another one piled on top, but hardly evidence that anything was wrong with their new dream house. The odd occurrences were beginning to add up, and each went noticed and was then dismissed. "Three different times within the last eight months, as I'm in the kitchen doing the dishes or making dinner before my husband gets home from work, I'd think to go into the living room to turn on the television. As I'd walk in, I'm not even a foot away from the entertainment center, and it turns on by itself. Once in awhile, if I have a very moody day and happen to be angry about something, light bulbs burn out at once. If I am very happy about something while driving, my car horn honks by itself," Deirdre says.

The oddest event happened in 2004. It was a dewy, dreary summer night, and Deidre and her husband were both watching television and relaxing. The heat and the mood eventually made Deirdre fall asleep, and when she woke up, she was disoriented.

"It was around 3:00 A.M. when I groggily awoke from a deep sleep because I sensed someone near the couch," she says. "This really tall man was standing right next to me and said, 'Oh, I'm going to the bathroom. I'll be right back.' Being half asleep as I was, I laid back down for five seconds, then got up from the sofa thinking that man was my husband and went into my bedroom. To my sleepy surprise, Todd was fast asleep in the bedroom. In fact, he was snoring. I remember wondering why he announced where he was going and how he had gotten back to sleep so quickly."

With her senses returning, Deirdre began to wonder what she had just seen. She woke up Todd, noticing he was deep in sleep, and asked him why he had woken her up and if he had just gone to the bathroom. His response, said in sleepy tones, made her mouth drop. He told her he had not done any such thing and that she should just go back to sleep.

Things started to make more sense the next day, and the pieces of the picture were coming together. "When I got up the next morning, I reflected back on my experience. Now fully awake, I realized what I had seen was in fact an apparition. It really scared the daylights out of me. I had never seen a ghost before in my life, and I knew it was a ghost because I remember it being whitish and a lot taller than my husband."

After experiencing so many things in the house, Deirdre still wonders why the ghost, existing on another plane or in another time, felt the need to make contact on that night and why such an ordinary event would be her proof of an afterlife. She is no longer frightened by what happened that night, and the house continues to suffer unexplained bumps. She has not seen her mysterious man again, however, and she is left with more questions than answers.

Linda

UNION CITY, NEW JERSEY

There are places people believe to be haunted. Cemeteries and buildings that have had some incident of disaster are prime suspects. College dorms, filled with students and urban legends, can always be counted on to be haunted. Then there are the places within your own house. Children cry about monsters under their beds or ghosts in the closet, but there is one room in the house people fear more than any other. Your basement is a dark and lonely place, the foundation of the house, usually reserved for storage and maybe a laundry machine. Some people have nice finished cellars or workshops built to pass the time, but in most homes, basements are like black holes. You rarely go down there, and the shadows are unfamiliar.

Something about them does not make you feel at ease. In Salem, Massachusetts, for example, many believe that their basements are haunted. There, unlike many towns and cities, there might be a reason for the hauntings. According to rumor, many poorer residents of the town are said to have buried their relatives in the dirt of the cellar after they changed the burial standards in the early twentieth century. It became very expensive to embalm and bury a loved ones, so they dug holes and hoped for the best. Union City, New Jersey, is far from Salem, but that does not make the basements there any less scary or any less haunted.

Laurie now investigates the paranormal and shares her stories freely with people. She no longer fears the unknown and confronts it head on. Her story began when she was a child. "When I was eight years old, I moved with my family to a two-story, two-family house in Union City, New Jersey. The house was 150 years old and nothing to brag about. The home was originally one story that had the second story added in 1951. We moved there in 1964. My stepfather renovated the house on the inside, and my folks and I lived upstairs, and my grandmother downstairs."

The house was not known to be haunted, not that she would have understood anything like that when she was young. There was one place in the house she hated to go. "There was a bluestone basement that was as big as the other floors of the house. It was cold no matter what the season and had only one window, which was small and at the street level. It was dark, except for the light fixtures my dad installed that consisted of a bare light bulb. There was one in the front of the cellar and one in the back, both with a pull chain. There was a switch at the top of the stairs that would turn on the light in the front, but if someone pulled the chain downstairs, the switch was useless."

She found ways to avoid the cellar, but there were times when she was forced to go down there. "We didn't have a dryer so we had a wash line in the basement to hang clothes when it rained and in winter time. Because my mother was in ill health and couldn't make two flights of stairs, I was stuck with the clothes-line detail.

"The first time I went down to fetch the clothes, I saw a sheet move on the line, and then I saw an apparition of a woman. I bolted for the stairs and ran to my mom, who said I was imagining things and sent me right back down there. I rushed as fast as I could, which afterwards became my usual speed routine for the clothes detail."

The woman was about thirty with long brown hair. She was of medium height, and Laurie describes her as being unattractive. She was wearing a long ivory-colored dress, but what Laurie really remembers is the angry expression the ghost had on her face, an emotion Laurie would sense from her often. Through the many times she saw the woman, her status in our world changed. Sometimes she was translucent, but other times she was solid, as if she still lived in the basement. Laurie is unsure, but thinking back, it seems she was more solid the angrier she was.

Over time, Laurie's feelings about the basement never changed, although she did eventually spend more time down there. "One day, I was getting the clothes, and a shoebox of candles fell from the rafters right onto my head. This startled me, and as I was picking up the candles, I heard a woman laughing. Again, my mom showed no sympathy and said her usual."

Seeing the woman became part of the routine. "I came to view the basement as my own personal hell. When I was eleven, my folks set up an area down there for me and my friends to hang out. This was very eventful, with objects coming out of the dark and hurling at our heads, mysterious laughter, and an occasional manifestation here and there. Luckily, she never came upstairs. She stayed mostly in the basement and occasionally appeared on the ground floor in the hallway. My house was not the popular hangout."

Some answers finally came, although they did not help to calm whatever was in the basement. "Finally, I started nosing around in the house's past history and used the antique Ouija board belonging to my grandma," Laurie says. "I learned that the woman's name was Linda. She was a suicide who had been stood up at the altar and had an abusive father. She caved under the whole trauma and killed herself in the basement." Laurie and her grandmother were able to get access to records that proved the story they got from the board. "Research on the house showed that a man with a daughter her age once lived there, and he sold wine from a wine cellar in the basement. There was a death record for the man who had the wine business but not for his daughter, which I found strange. Her name was Linda, as the Ouija board had told us."

The story gave them a reason and age, and maturity led to her finally confronting the spirit. When she was fourteen, the light in the basement would not work, and as she went down the stairs, a colander her grandmother kept on the wall fell and tripped her up. As she lay hurt at the bottom of the stairs, she again heard the laughter. For the first time, she was angry instead of scared. "I told her in my own fourteen-year-old way that she was not going to terrorize me anymore and that she needed to go to the light. Then my grandmother went down there and pretty much did the same thing. She never really left, but she did stop the attacks."

The Message

MIDDLETON, NEW JERSEY

Middleton, New Jersey, is the town immortalized in the movies of Kevin Smith and made famous in the working-class rock music produced by Jon Bon Jovi, one of its famous sons. People there are blue collar or first-generation white collar, and the town, like many suburbs, is beginning to lose its identity as parts of town become more affluent. It is the picture of a typical Northeast suburb, and the people there do not think about ghosts. Even a town like this is not immune to the paranormal. The supernatural has a habit of slipping in everywhere, telling us the appearance of a ghost is not always the result of looking.

We have a hard time letting go sometimes, even when it is for the best. A ghost may try to make his presence known to tell us to move on, but we ignore the signs and linger on, not understanding the things happening around us. John was trying desperately to get someone to listen to him, and after his friends and fiancée turned him away, he turned to Denise. All he wanted to say was that he was all right.

John was known as a good, typical guy who graduated from high school and then went straight to work. In the fall of 1997, he asked his girlfriend, Tara, to marry him. She said yes, and three weeks later, he passed away for reasons that have not been discovered to this day.

Denise, Tara's roommate and best friend, went home with her just days after she got the news. Maybe it was how likable he was or maybe it was the way he went with no explanation, but the passing unsettled everyone John had touched.

Unusual things started to happen the night of his wake. Everyone was standing in the driveway getting ready to leave, and the motion sensor lights began to blink on and off. John had been working on them when he died, but he hadn't finished installing them. "They had never worked before, and never did again," says Denise.

Then Tara became convinced that she saw John at night. "She would wake up and see him sitting on the bean bag in her room," Denise recalls. She would also see him at the foot of her bed and hear him walking through the house. She would be too scared to talk to him and lie under the covers, hysterical. She began sleeping in her parents' bed and was unable to walk in areas of the house where she thought John had walked. Her parents thought she might have post-traumatic stress disorder (PTSD), but they still ripped up the carpet and changed the house around to settle her mind. Nothing worked.

In the meantime, John's friends started to see him at night, too. He would appear at night at the foot of their beds or in the corner of the room. He always seemed like he wanted to communicate with them. Most of them hid under the covers until he disappeared, or they ran out of their rooms at the first sight of their old friend. The figure was not doing anything scary or intimidating; he just wasn't supposed to be there. Others convinced themselves that they were dreaming until they started to talk about it. He appeared to at least six of his friends before one of their mothers went to a psychic about it. The psychic said he was trying to tell them something, and they went to her as a group. They were unable to make contact.

Denise also had her own experience, but she didn't tell anyone until eight months later, when Tara decided to go back to school at Lynchburg College in Lynchburg, West Virginia. Tara asked Denise about her memories of the wake and the funeral because she had blocked out most of them. Denise told her the details and then began to tell her a dream she'd had not long after John's death.

"I call it a dream because I don't have any other explanation," Denise says. She was sleeping in her bed completely in the dark when she was suddenly awoken. John was standing in the middle of her room looking down on her. Everything in the room was dark except for him. He had on a navy blue polo shirt with a red symbol and glasses, something she had never seen him wear. "He told me to tell Tara that he was okay, that he was happy, that he had moved on, and that she doesn't have to be afraid." Denise says he was solid, talked in his usual voice, and there was nothing unusual other than that she knew he was dead and the dead aren't supposed to talk.

Tara's reaction when Denise told her about this was even stranger. She ran out of the room and came back with the only possessions she kept from John—a navy blue polo shirt with a red rider and a pair of glasses he never wore after he had gotten his contacts.

There were no more occurrences after that. After hearing the story, John's friends moved on knowing their buddy was okay. Tara found peace, as well. "Prior to that, she used to go to his grave every single day," Denise says. "It was an obsession, and she felt she had to go. If she didn't, she couldn't function." Now she is married to another man and is happy in her life.

"After my dream, the message got to her."

Whispers

PITTSBURGH, PENNSYLVANIA

Some people live through hauntings for years. They become part of their lives, and outsiders can never understand. A house becomes like a heartbeat, thumping normally and then spiking every once in a while. Every so often, even though they have become used to sharing their residence with another resident, something happens that makes them gasp. Sometimes even the normal paranormal becomes abnormal.

The hauntings began early for Emily. "I was eight years old and visiting my grandmother's house outside of Pittsburgh, and it was bedtime for me. My mother and grandmother were in the finished basement of the house, and the bedrooms were on the third [floor]. I climbed the stairs to the bedroom and got into bed with my grandmother's cat.

"I was just falling asleep when I heard someone open and close the door to the basement and begin to climb the two-story staircase to the third floor. Assuming it was my mother coming to bed, I called out to her and got no response. I felt a little uneasy and got out of bed, left the bedroom, and went to the landing of the third-floor staircase. I could hear my mother's footfalls coming closer and waited for her to round the final set of stairs before facing me on the landing directly below me. When my mother rounded the corner, I realized something very weird had happened. She was not there. No one came around the bend to face me, and the footsteps stopped. At the same moment, my grandmother's cat flung herself off the landing, screeching and batting at the air as she hurled herself down the staircase."

Emily had good reason to be scared. The house had its share of reasons for a haunting, and over the years, people had reported unexplained things in every room in the house. Emily had never heard the stories as a child but had her own reasons for being scared. "My grandmother's house had always spooked me. It was a funeral home in the fifties, and my grandfather, a mortician, died in the house. That was the first of many subsequent unexplained incidents there."

The phantoms in the house made themselves known often, but it is the variety of the experiences she remembers today. "I've heard singing and seen shadowy people in corners. Sometimes, the piano would bang a single key once or twice. I felt the ghosts were friendly, and were both female and male. My great-grandmother, a real character, also died in the house. I always suspected my grandfather might have caused some of the activity."

Eventually, the house was put on the market because her grandmother became too old to care for it. She relocated to a retirement community nearby, and the ghost seemed to follow her there. "I knew she hated to leave her house. She fell on her hip in the new place and wasn't found for a couple of days. She was admitted into a local hospital, and we came in from New Jersey to see her, staying overnight in her new place. We settled in but were very tired and soon planned out our sleeping arrangements. My mother took the bedroom, and my husband and I slept on the sofa bed in the living room where my grandmother had fallen."

After years of experiencing ghosts, Emily thought she had put all of that behind her. Although the retirement home was not nearly as homey, it was ghost-free. That was until they fell asleep. "About 2:30 A.M., I was awakened by a raspy breathing, in and out. It was very loud and sounded like it came from all areas of the room, like surround-sound stereo. The breathing sound was oppressive and paralyzed me with fear. It wouldn't stop, and I had my eyes clamped shut. I was afraid if I opened them I'd see what was making the noise."

Unlike the ghosts they were used to, there seemed to be something dark and evil about this spirit. The difference attacked her senses. "A smell of body odor, sweat, and sawdust started to fill my nose. It was overpowering."

She felt helpless and alone, even with her husband next to her. She finally was able to move and tried to wake him up. He would not rouse, and she lay there, asking whatever it was to leave. Eventually, she fell asleep, but she does not remember the feeling going away before she drifted off.

"When I woke up the next morning, everything was normal, but I just sat up in bed staring at every corner, wondering whether I had dreamed the whole thing. My mom came out of the bedroom, and I told her what had happened. She became very emotional and said that her father had always smelled like that when he came home from work. My mom was convinced it was my grandfather's spirit."

To this day, she does not understand why her grandfather would come back as such an intimidating spirit, especially when he had not been that type of person in real life, and the ghosts she had experienced in the old house had never harmed her. She admits it may have been the strength of the smell that made her feel it was evil and that whatever was in the room with her was not trying to do her harm.

The experience did not end there. "My husband woke up while we were talking and said, 'Wait, that wasn't you last night? I thought you were trying to bug me by breathing loudly in my ear.'"

The Most Haunted House in the Country

The old house at 1129 Ridge Avenue in Pittsburgh has a reputation the town wishes it could lose. For years it was considered the most haunted house in the country. The legend begins with a murder. The original owner of the house, Charles Wright Congelier, was thought to be having an affair with his maid, Essie. His wife found out about it and stabbed him to death and decapitated his presumed lover.

It did not take long for the ghost stories to start. Railroad workers who used the building some years later moved out after hearing weeping and crying at night. Then in 1901, a doctor conducted experiments on women, cutting off their heads and seeing how long they would live. Five women were discovered dead, although the death toll was estimated to be higher, and people began to whisper about something evil within the walls urging people to kill. It existed like that for many years, alternating between bizarre, deadly accidents and reports of lights, screams, and sobs in the dark.

In 1927, the house was destroyed by a nearby explosion that left the surrounding buildings untouched. The house was never rebuilt, but some of the spirits have stayed around.

CHAPTER 6

GHOST STORIES OF THE SOUTH

Things happen a bit slower in the South. Perhaps it's the heat that makes people more laid-back, more deliberate with their movements and thoughtful of their energy. If the Northeast ghosts are born of Native Americans, the South has its share of Civil War ghosts in towns burned down by Union soldiers and never-forgotten battlefields. A strong religious community paints the paranormal with a wide brush. Ghosts are evil, often tools of the Devil, and to see one is to some-how be touched. It is a generalization, like anything said about a whole area, but the ideas help to teach people in the South what ghosts are. Not all of these stories are about evil occurrences, but there is an element of the dark side in them all.

Faye

SALISBURY, MARYLAND

Can a person change after he dies? Traditional paranormal investigators say no. A ghost is the person he was before he died, and there is no revelation in death that magically makes bad people good. This theory is not backed up by some hauntings people have reported, though. While it may be true that a ghost is the same person she was before she passed, there are many stories of ghosts moving on after they have come to terms with something or fixing something they did wrong in life. It might be only a romantic notion, but there might be some kind of perspective gained. As the living, we hope our sins will be washed away.

Faye was not a well-liked person in life. She was a typical old person of the Eastern Shore, not stupid by any means but very set in her ways, and it comes as no surprise that those ways went back several generations. While there is no one around to document her early life, near the end, she was known as a pain, and people avoided her. Pictures show that she had been an attractive woman in her youth, but the cancer she suffered through robbed her of her looks and rotted her disposition. Even her husband, Clayton, sick from his own illnesses, had a hard time defending her, although he dearly loved her. As her life slipped away, she got nastier and less tolerable. Toward the end, all those around her had trouble dealing with her and avoided her. This did nothing to change her disposition, and things got worse.

Ben was supposed to be able to handle her type. He had recently started as a caregiver to the elderly, and he had all the technical skills to work for the couple. "When I met my partner, his friend had two elderly parents who needed to be watched over during the day, and I volunteered," he says. "Faye was a very old-looking woman who had been sent home from the hospital because there was no treatment possible to make her final days on earth better. Clayton was not supposed to walk, and I was assigned to take care of them and make sure he didn't walk around and complicate his leg problem."

There was not enough time to introduce himself and get used to the old couple. Three hours into the assignment, Faye gave into her disease and died in the kitchen. After that, Ben decided the work was not for him and left to find another career. Three years later, Clayton died, as well. He had been living in the house since his wife's death, and when he passed, Ben and his roommate moved in. It took a while, but they started to remove the items the couple had collected over the years, selling them in auctions and yard sales and giving the money to the couple's estate.

Once the items were out, things began to happen. "We had set up our computers, and after, my front light would turn on and off." They did not think anything of it, and asked someone to come in and check out the wiring in the house. He was unable to find anything wrong, and Ben began to think that the ghost of one of the elderly couple was making life hard for them. This is a common theme in the paranormal world. Two of the most widely known catalysts for a haunting are the renovation of an old house and the moving out of a person's possessions. Both disrupt the known world for the spirit, and may even seem criminal to the ghost if he doesn't know he is dead.

Ben, unlike many who experience a restless spirit, was quick to act. "I said to them, 'Okay, I understand, but please don't mess up the computer.'" Other things started to happen, and as with many paranormal situations, the animal of the house was the most in tune with what was happening. "Our cat would walk into the living room, look at me in my rocking chair, and suddenly my computer would turn on. I bought a new base with the switches under the monitor, and it kept happening."

Without anything more being said, the ghost and the roommate reached a calm balance in the house. Things still happened, but there was a different tone in the air. "While I would play my guitar in the front room, I could see someone out of the corner of my eye. When I turned, no one was there. This was not a shadow but a full person."

He had never talked to his roommate, Ed, about the apparition until he started to have his ghostly audience. When he finally came forward, he was surprised by Ed's response. "He said it was Faye because he had seen her several times. I accepted it, and was really happy she seemed to have fun. After a lifetime of being called a naughty name, I hope she was happy on earth for once."

The spirit continued to listen to him play, but it was not until the spring that Ben truly realized she was a different person. "I was doing dishes while Ed watched TV. Our cat walked over to the kitchen entrance, and I turned around to say hi to her. When I did, all the kitchen cabinets opened and closed. I stood there as the cat's look seemed to say, 'Didn't you see that coming?' I dried my hands and sat down in my chair and told Faye she got me good." Despite the intensity of the scene, Ben feels she was playing a joke on him and not trying to scare him.

Things went along that way for a while. She made herself known by playing with anything electronic in the house and was seen out of the corner of eyes. Eventually the owner told them they needed to buy the house or move out. "We bought another house, and my last time in the empty place, I invited Faye with us." Their new house has its share of haunted occurrences, and Ben thinks Faye is there and has found some friends in death. At the very least, the old hag has found a friend in the living.

The Real Haunted House

Salisbury is the home of a staged haunted house known throughout the surrounding towns, but another dwelling in town has raised eyebrows as being the home to real ghosts. Known as the Hotel Ester, this large residence on Church Street has been the subject of rumor and urban legend. Online reports say it was originally a home for a retired doctor, and out of the goodness of his heart, the man began taking in patients who could not make their way to any of the hospitals in the surrounding towns. Eventually it was expanded, and as it grew, it looked more like a haunted house, and then it eventually became a retirement home.

Unexplained fires continue to break out in the building, and people inside have heard screams and insane laughter. People go by and see lights flicker, especially the outside lights, or they see dark figures walking through the outside walls to seek shelter inside. While some may attribute the hauntings to any of the patients or elderly who may have died in the hospital, most believe the activity is due to John Thanos, a killer who once lived there. Thanos was an unstable man who murdered three teens and then shocked the state by saying he would raise them from the grave so he could kill them again. This dark figure could be enough to draw negative energy to the house.

The Unwanted Playmate

SHREVEPORT, LOUISIANA

Little children are the wild cards in the paranormal. Their stories stay with us and make the hairs on our arms stand on end. However unfortunate, we can understand an apparition of our grandmother coming to see us. She might be a ghost, but she lived a full life. Children point at tragedy, and seeing a ghost of a little boy in your room telling you something bad happened to him might be too much to handle. Childlike ghosts present some of the most disturbing ghost tales, and witnesses are always affected by their run-ins with a spritely spook. They also seem to be more numerous than other types of ghosts. Whether the witness sees the apparition or just hears a child giggling or crying, these apparitions are spoken of more often. Some have theorized that all children who die have the possibility to be ghosts. In addition to having an unfulfilled life and more energy, they might not know the rules of the dead and just play when they can.

Kristina lived in a historic home in the third-largest city in Louisiana. The city is often the site of movie sets, but there has never been a good ghost movie that takes place there. Kristina's house would be a good set. It was built in the early 1900s and was once the house of the state's governor. There is a historical marker out front, sealing its historical importance to the town and the state. The inside was modern and not looking for something from the past to show itself. There had been rumors of a ghost in the house, but she was not thinking about anything paranormal that afternoon.

"I remember sitting on a chair watching TV one day. It was nothing scary, just a regular daytime show," she says. "It was bright and sunny outside. It was sometime between 11:00 A.M. and 2:00 P.M. The way our living room was set up, our couch was in front of a big bay window. To the right of the couch, in the middle of the room, was a chair, which I was sitting in, and to the left was our TV. I kept waiting for my boyfriend or my roommate to come home because I was getting pretty bored, and there was nothing to do and nothing on TV."

She was about to shut off the television when she spotted something out of the corner of her eye. "I thought I saw something on the couch, but when I turned to look, it was gone. We did not have any pets that could have been jumping or playing around. A few minutes later, the same thing happened. I saw something out of the corner of my eye, but when I turned to look, it was gone. I was a little bit freaked out, but I knew that I was not going crazy. I knew that I had seen something there. I also knew that my house was haunted, and I felt like whoever haunted my house was there in the room with me."

This happened several more times, making her more uncomfortable each time whatever was there made itself known. She wondered what it was she was seeing. "As I sat in my chair thinking about all this, I thought to myself that if it happened again I would turn my head slowly and see if I could catch a glimpse of whatever it was." When it happened a few minutes later, she slowly turned her head and saw him.

"I saw him so clearly that I will never forget this. It was a small child no more than about thirteen. He was wearing a white shirt, a brown vest, some brown knickers, white socks, brown shoes, and a brown hat. He had blond hair and freckles. That is how close I was to him. I actually saw the freckles on his face." She remembers thinking that the boy looked as if he had stepped out of an old movie and that there was something about him that made him feel out of time.

"I got chills." Kristina was most thrown off by the fact that the ghost was a child. "I think I was expecting something different, maybe someone older. Once he realized that I was looking right at him, he vanished. I believe that he was definitely more frightened of me than I was of him, and that is why he disappeared. I don't think he had actually expected me to see him."

The feeling went away, and she never saw the little boy again. Theories abound as to why there are so many reports of the ghosts of children. Some feel there is something about their energy, untapped by a short life, that allows them to return. Others feel the death of a child is always connected to tragedy and therefore the spirit always has a reason to return. Michael Markowicz, a paranormal investigator and an expert on EVPs, has another possible reason. He has collected hundreds of recordings of ghost children and feels that souls on the other side have to live by rules.

"Maybe that's why we don't see them all the time. They're only allowed to make contact when they are supposed to, when there is a reason for it. That's why I have so many recordings of children. They don't know the rules or don't care. They're too busy being kids," he says. Markowicz has even recorded older spirits telling the children not to talk or to stop playing around.

Kristina feels that her little ghost had a motive. "I think he was bored and wanted company. He felt that I knew he was there and that I was okay with it. I feel like since this has happened there is no doubt in my mind of what is out there. I always knew there were spirits or ghosts, but when you actually see it with your own eyes, you have a feeling of just knowing." Her little spirit may continue to be restless and unable to find peace, and that makes the whole visit heartbreaking. That is what she remembers when she remembers the ghostly boy.

Sneaking in the Back Door

EAST TEXAS

People in Texas are not as believing as other people in the country. They have their local legends and folklore, but haunted houses are for people in the North. There is a sense of history there, but it is different from other parts of the country. Connection to relatives is more like tradition. Their faith allows for the attack of demons and the belief that the church can help them, but not ghosts. And never are the ghosts family members. When you hear a story, you have to stop and listen and believe it to be true.

Rebecca had a connection to her family. After her parents retired, they moved to a track of land that had been handed down through the generations. "We were staying at my parents' retirement home in the country. The original home of my great-grandparents is less than fifty feet from the new home that my parents built for their retirement. Up the hill is the family-founded church and cemetery. To come from town up the road to get to my great-granny's home, it's much easier to cross the field, now occupied by my mother's home. Drunken and sober relatives for over a hundred years would use this path to come from town or other family dwellings to get to my granny's house.

"I was playing hooky from church. My husband was with me, and while my parents were still at church, we were getting dressed to go out to lunch. My mother had a habit of calling out my name when she would be coming in the door. As I was in the hallway bathroom fixing my hair with the door open, I distinctly heard rather loudly my name being called out as to get my attention. I stepped out to see if I needed to unlock the door. No one was there. I checked the door, garage, and driveway. No Mom. I was merely puzzled and went back to what I was doing.

"Not five seconds passed and again, loudly to get my attention, my name was called out. Not just my first name, which is three syllables, but also my middle name. Clear as a bell." She left the room and looked around the corner. There was no one there, although she had a view of the house and the driveway from where she was. No one could have entered the house without her seeing. She asked her husband if he had called her or heard anything. He said no. "My husband doesn't even come close to sounding like my mom's high singsong voice. As a matter of fact, if it had been him, he wouldn't have used my middle name." Everyone was at church. They were alone in the house.

Her parents were not surprised when she told them. They had been having weird things happen in the house since they had moved in. There would be knocking on doors with no one there. It was more intense for Rebecca. "I would feel fear and really didn't like sleeping there. I felt as if I were being watched. But it's my mom and dad. I went anyway. When I visit now, I sleep with a fan on for white noise. I leave the TV on when I am alone there."

Her son moved in with her parents while he went to a local college. He had also felt the ghosts in the house. "On one visit, he took me aside to tell me he saw something that was very unusual. He had seen it out of the corner of his eye. A man in a 1940s-style zoot suit was walking across the front yard, as if he just walked through the center of the house at an angle. I had never told my son about his great-grandfather or the voice that I had heard. I let him know that his great-grandfather would often come home from a night of drinking and try to sneak in the back door.

My great-granny would leave the light on so he would not miss the house."

The night trips went beyond seeing the man cross the yard. "After my parents moved into their home, my mother would often see the light on in the old house across the yard. I told her there was no way, but she would say that she would see it often late at night. I never pointed out to her that there had been no live electricity to the house for twenty years."

Rebecca finally shared the story with other members of her family. She felt she was the only one who experienced things, and she was beginning to wonder whether it had something to do with her immediate family. People who make contact with ghosts often feel as if they are alone, which is one of the reasons they stay silent about what has happened to them. Her cousin actually confirmed the hauntings. "He let me know that the family has been spotting a spirit for over fifty years or more walking that path."

Although she still is reluctant to visit the house, the stories of the night walks hold a much different meaning for her. "I grew up visiting this farm and land, and to me, it had so much meaning. Over the years, this has helped me understand my long-gone relatives and their lives they lived. I believe that as an adopted child, I always felt like I didn't have family waiting on the other side for me. I didn't feel like I was looked upon as part of the real family. I think that I was being told that I was a part of it all. I feel so much a part of the family and the land itself. I don't feel like I am just an outsider. I wasn't sure I would want the land after my parents' death. But I feel like no one else should have it, and it belongs to me and I to it." For Rebecca, seeing the dead ended up being her link to life.

Dark Things in the Apartment

DALLAS, TEXAS

No one is sure if a ghost is attracted to a person or if certain people are just designed to observe the other side. Most have only one chance to see a ghost, and they may be the lucky ones. Many do not have their first experience until later in life, but often one encounter acts as the jump-start for more. The flood gates open up, and people find the number of ghosts and the sheer volume of the hauntings overwhelming. There is the rare occasion when a combination of people open the door. They become the tumblers falling just the right way.

Beth and Stacey have had many experiences together, and the young ladies believe it is due to their astrological signs. Beth is a Pisces, the last sign in the zodiac, and Stacey is an Aries, the first. Together, according to people they have spoken to in the astrological field, they form a life cycle. This makes them a magnet for all sorts of paranormal activity, although they have never received a good reason why this is. All they know is that all of the apartments they've shared together have been haunted, and while most of their adventures have been exciting and harmless, something evil attracted to their energy found an entrance in the summer of 1994.

The summer after Beth's freshman year in college, they rented a one-bedroom apartment in Dallas, Texas. The rent was right, and even though it was in a hard neighborhood, they never felt threatened because of the people constantly in and out of their place. Knowing their history together, they waited for something unexplainable to happen.

They did not have to wait long. "It was really benevolent," says Beth. The spirit would try to help them but could never quite get it right. It would take the batteries out of the remote control and replace them with fresh ones. It would put soda in the freezer to get it cold, but they would find it only after the can had exploded. It would turn lights off when they weren't home. They had gotten used to the little annoyances when they accidentally invited something else in.

When they moved in, Stacey had put crystals in the entrances to protect them and keep bad spirits out. She placed one by the front door and another in the window in the back. Beth came across the one near the door while cleaning one day and threw it on the counter. Almost at once, the atmosphere in the apartment changed.

"You could feel the difference," she says. "Nothing had happened yet, but the mood was off. Friends came and went very quickly. They would call us later and tell us it had felt weird and they had needed to get air. I didn't understand it at all. I thought maybe they felt the stress we were both feeling from working too much."

Two days later, they were getting ready to go to bed. They slept in the same bed, and as Beth put her head down, she noticed a black shadow behind the television facing them. She tried to ignore it, but soon Stacey asked her if she could see something in the corner of the room.

The object was as tall as the ceiling and four feet wide. At first it looked like a shadow, but the only light came from the television. It began to move toward them, and as it got closer, it appeared to have substance, more like thick, black smoke than a shadow. There was no sound coming from it, and it did not give off an odor, but they could tell it was real and that it was not there to be helpful.

"Negative. I want to say evil, but at that point, I didn't sense that. It was just negative, like anger or bad feelings." Stacey ran to put the light on, and it flew across the room to intercept her. She got the light on and ran back to the bed, but the cloud followed her and stood at the foot of the bed. Although it had no eyes, they knew it was looking at them.

The dark figure was right in front of them, and they could see it fully. It would start to creep onto the bed and then creep back when they would yell at it to stop. They were both scared. The cloud was both threatening and mesmerizing, as the streams of smoke that made it up moved like a lava lamp and then bled into one another. "You felt that it could possess you at any moment. We wanted to look away but couldn't."

After fifteen minutes of watching this, they called Stacey's cousin, Brandy. She was psychic and had experience dealing with the paranormal. She came over a few minutes later with a camera, a picture of her spirit guide, batteries, a bell, and a piece of fabric that Beth does not remember the significance of.

They bolted from the bed and got the door when she arrived. They had to walk straight through the figure to unlock the door. "You could feel it. It sort of sapped you or something. It was weird," she says. They ran back into the bedroom, but Brandy stopped right in the doorway, consumed by the smoke. She wouldn't move. "It was like she was doped or something." When she eventually got into the room, she tried to load the batteries into the camera, but they were dead.

Brandy began to ring her bell, and the spirit moved out of the bedroom. They shut the door, but the image of the object was coming through the wood. It started to flash images on it, and all three of them began to draw what they were seeing. The first was a face with a three-point crown. It also spelled out the words *sex* and *ept*. Beth saw all the images in black, and Stacey saw them in white, but they were seeing the same thing.

Then Stacey started to act unusual. She would fade out and then complain about a stabbing pain in her back. Brandy tried different things to force the spirit back, but the more she tried, the harder Stacey yelled.

The cloud eventually moved out into the living room and then slowly disappeared, but they felt it never left.

After that night, Beth and Stacey had a string of bad luck involving their jobs and love lives. Everyone who would come into the apartment would freak out and want to leave. A friend who spent the night on the couch said he heard whispers in his ear all night long. A few weeks later, they decided to move out and head back to college early.

"We just sold everything, packed up, and left," Beth says. Nothing ever happened to the couple again, and eventually they went their own ways. Both have seen ghosts since then but nothing as intense as the dark figure who found a home in their apartment. It took their energy at that location to invite him in.

The Phantom Horse

PHARR, TEXAS

Pharr, Texas, is a town on the Mexican border that prides itself on the multicultural diversity of the town. There is a legend there, passed by locals, about a ghost horse who rides near an old barn. The use of the barn is lost to the town now, but the legend is still passed from believer to nonbeliever and back to believer. Many can accept the idea of a ghost in their house, but an animal trapped in time is more confusing. From house pets to beasts from the sea, phantom animals are a growing part of the paranormal.

Michael first learned about the ghost horse when he and his friends were out with some girls from the town. He was a believer in the supernatural, but he did not believe the story they were telling about a spectral horse that appeared and disappeared while spectators watched. "We both thought it was nonsense at the time, but since it was a secluded area, and being teenage boys, we saw it as an opportunity to check the place out."

The horse could be seen in a brushy area near a small electrical facility. It had been spotted for years, but part of the legend said it appeared only when people were not looking for it. They made their way out to the location, thinking more about the girls than the beast. The road that led up to the building had a channel on one side and an abandoned farm on the other. The unpaved road fed into the parking lot, but the building, surrounded by an expanse of brush and mesquite trees, was locked down for the night.

"We waited for what seemed an eternity, and I remember coming to the conclusion that they were probably seeing a real horse that lived on the farm. One of the girls exclaimed that it was not a real horse because horses are not supposed to vanish in front of people's eyes. For some reason or another, the ghost horse did not grace us with his presence this night."

Michael forgot about the legend, but it came up again when a friend came to visit near Halloween. The spirit of the holiday got the better of them, and they decided to give the ghost horse one more chance to make itself known. "I can remember it was rather breezy that night, and I thought I had never seen the clouds hang so low. It seemed as if they were just above the tree. I will also always remember the moon."

They were about halfway down the road when they spotted something outside the passenger window. "I realized that it was the form of the head of a huge stallion. Suddenly the rest of the body began to materialize. I remember screaming, 'Look, the ghost!' Everyone in the car witnessed it galloping on the road right beside us. This was the biggest and most beautiful horse I had ever seen. It galloped at the same speed as our vehicle and seemed almost as if the horse were riding with us. Its long hair was flowing in the moonlight. This horse was very muscular, and I could see the definition of his body as he moved gracefully about two feet from my side. It looked like it was a film projection from the past, some type of physical recording or impression that had found a way to replay itself for one reason or another. It was somewhat transparent."

The horse rode alongside them and then passed in front of the car and disappeared. They waited for the animal to come back, but it never returned. They were at a loss to explain what they had seen. They assumed it was a wild horse, somehow let loose in the woods of what was left of the nearby farm, but that did not account for its coming out of nowhere and vanishing before their eyes. Although there was thick brush all over the property, they never saw it go into the brush or into the trees. It was just there and then gone.

Another time, Michael saw the apparition near the facility instead of on the road. "We had already been waiting for him for quite some time, and we had begun to grow impatient. We heard some movement in the brush. We turned to see the horse galloping though the mesquite trees before vanishing once again right before our eyes. We could see beyond the brush where the horse had appeared, but we could not see or hear anything running afterwards. He had pulled one of his disappearing acts once again."

He went back several times, trying to re-create what had happened before. He met with no success until he went back to the plant, this time with a female friend who had not heard the myth. The phantom again came into view. "She became very frightened and pointed out to me that she could clearly see the figure of a horse grazing in the distance. This time, the horse was different. He was in a shadow form, and he was completely dark. I could clearly see the outline of a horse, but the figure did not have any features even though he was close enough that any features could have been easily made out."

The apparition was grazing a few dozen feet away. Michael got out of the car and began to walk toward the animal. "He looked up and looked me dead in the eye. Even though I could not actually see his eyes, I knew for certain he was glaring right at me. The ghostly form fixated on me for a few more moments then galloped off in the opposite direction."

Some who study the supernatural might say he had seen a psychic recording, a memory somehow trapped in time, but Michael saw intelligence in the beast. "I got the feeling the horse had become familiar with me and maybe even possibly remembered me."

He never saw it after that. Since Michael's last sighting, people have fenced off the property, closing off the stretch of land where the horse was most seen and perhaps interrupting the energy flow that allowed the ghost to be seen. It might be that fewer people have been around to see the horse.

"I don't know for certain," says Michael. "He could have moved to those greener pastures in the sky."

Haunted Sleepy Hollow and the Ghost Dog

The ghosts of animals are nothing new to the paranormal field, and large, black dogs are some of the scariest. According to myth, these dogs were supposed to be the harbinger of bad things, and seeing them meant death to the witness. Other stories claim they are the employees of the Devil himself. Most of the reports of these odd animals are cases of misidentification. Different parts of the country have wild dogs, wolves, or coyotes, and they are not seen often enough for people to truly appreciate their size and behavior. Some reports are too unusual to be explained away, and these animals are anything but natural.

In a section of Prospect, Kentucky, known as Sleepy Hollow, there are reports of a demonic dog. Stories of it scatter the Internet, sometimes changing the location to several other areas in Kentucky with the same name. The reports are a smorgasbord of sightings, ranging from a three-legged canine to a large, werewolf-like monster with wings.

There are true reports of the animal, and there are things about it that make it feel more like a ghost than a monster. People feel eyes on them as they travel the street. The animal appears and disappears as it tries to cross the road. In almost all of the reports, the animal has red eyes, although some have said the eyes began as yellow and changed to red.

The dog never harms anyone, but some associate it with several other hauntings in the area. There is a ghost car seen on one of the roads, and many believe the dog was a passenger during an ill-fated trip.

The Ghost of the Traveling Pants

HOLIDAY, FLORIDA

Laurie's work as a paranormal investigator sometimes forces her to keep quiet around people she does not know. Many investigators are fine among their own kind, but the outside world is not so accepting. Spending too much time with people who believe in the paranormal makes you think everyone is open about that kind of thing. It only takes a few people giving you that look, the one that says they will not invite you over for coffee sometime, to keep your stories and your ideas to yourself.

Holiday, Florida, is like that. On the west coast of Florida, halfway down the state but a world away from the lights of Orlando or the history of St. Petersburg, the town is bursting with untold ghost stories and legends. It just takes time and the right questions to get them out of people.

Laurie was not sure how her neighbors would perceive her experiences when she moved there. "When I first moved to this neighborhood, I kept a low profile. No one even knew I was a ghost hunter for ten years. Over those ten years, I heard lots of stories from neighbors about strange happenings around there, and since my ghost hunting pastime became known I have heard even more endless reports."

One story stays with her. "About twenty years ago, I went to a barbecue at a neighbor's home, a fisherman who had lots of local yokel buddies. Someone started telling a story saying that he had seen a pair of pants with shoes, like a man from the waist down, run across a nearby road on a rainy night. Another man jumped in to say that he saw it, too, and pretty soon they were comparing notes, and even with all I have seen and heard myself, I chalked this up to just too much beer and a bunch of tall-tale fishermen telling yet another ridiculous tale."

The story was a legend in the town, but like a lot of legends, there was an air of truth to it. While many accounts came secondhand, there also were people who saw the mysterious pants with their own eyes, making the other stories more believable. Laurie saw the story as legend, but a while later, she was confronted herself.

"About two years later," Laurie says, "I was coming home from a friend's home. It was late, and it was raining. There was a slight fog but nothing blinding. I saw my neighbor's eighteen-year-old son on the side of the highway near the road that leads to my road. His motorcycle had broken down, and he was soaked to the gills. I picked him up to give him a ride home, as he lived four houses down from me.

"We were driving down the road that eventually dead-ends to my road, and as we came over a rise and into the dip that followed, I could not believe what I saw. I was driving my old Bronco, which was very tall, and I had my high beams on, which illuminated the road for quite a distance. There are no streetlights here, and the road is very dark at night. The rain was still coming down but only a light drizzle now compared to the earlier downpour. There, about thirty yards in front of my truck, was what appeared to be a man from the waist down, crossing the road into a nearby trailer park." The ghost had no upper body, and she could not see its feet. There was only a pair of pants, suspended in midair.

"I locked my brakes and sat in disbelief and looked over to the boy beside me. He looked scared to death and asked me if I had seen what he had seen. I said that of course I had, and he replied, 'I am so glad. I have seen it before, and no one would have believed me, so I never told anyone.'"

The clothes matched the description given by the men at the barbecue. "The pants were brown, uniform-style pants, with shoes and a belt, but there was absolutely nothing visible of the man above the belt."

Although it seems that most towns in America have some kind of highway haunting, they are usually full-bodied apparitions, not just a pair of slacks. In fact, it is unusual to see only the clothes of a ghost. Many people feel that spirits can exists after death, but one of the questions always asked is why they have clothes. That question cannot be answered. But perhaps somehow their remaining energy consists of how they viewed themselves in life. Regardless, the phantom pants are a rarity in the field, even to someone with Laurie's resume.

The experience made Laurie more open to legends and local folklore. "That evening, I learned that no matter how ridiculous something sounds to me, I have to give the benefit of the doubt to people. I have heard several bizarre claims since. I can honestly say that even though I scoffed and shook my head when I heard the tale, I now have to eat my words on the ghost of the traveling pants. I have no explanation for what I saw that night. I haven't seen it again even though others claim to have."

Haunted Roads: Resurrection Mary

The most famous of all the roadside terrors is Resurrection Mary in Chicago, Illinois. The ghost, seen by dozens of travelers over the years, is supposed to be the spirit of a young woman who was hit by a car while hitchhiking home after a long night in a local dance club. She has been seen on the side of the road, dressed all in white, and has been picked up by helpful drivers. She disappears when they reach a local cemetery where she is supposed to be buried. People have had conversations with her only to have her dissolve in front of them. Others have seen her in the area of the cemetery, where she walks through the gate and dissolves.

Florida's Haunted Hotel

ST. PETERSBURG, FLORIDA

Haunted hotels throughout the country offer you a chance to stay and see a ghost for yourself. They advertise that spirits stay there, and you can, too. Most make their living on getting you in so that you can see them for yourself, and the people who stay, already in the mood to be scared, are not disappointed. The witnesses are more than happy to share what has happened to them. They have nothing to lose. A professional athlete, someone in the public eye and paid to have all his senses about him, might be less likely to come forward.

Unless they are trying to raise attention to promote a new paranormal project, people in the media rarely mention ghosts. It is not good for their images. For years, baseball players had been quiet about the activity in St. Petersburg's Renaissance Vinoy Hotel. The luxury hotel, located in one of Florida's most populous cities, has been the source of hushed tones for years, but once the reports starting seeing the light of day, baseball players from around the league began speaking up.

Dan Gordon and Mickey Bradley documented different tales of the paranormal in their book, *Haunted Baseball: Ghosts, Curses, Legends, and Other Eerie Events*, and had to include perhaps the most famous recent stories connected to athletics. According to their book, Scott Williamson, a pitcher for the Cincinnati Reds at the time, experienced a typical old hag incident and then saw an apparition of a man in his late thirties or early forties. ESPN caught on to the story, and pretty soon other ballplayers began coming forward with their stories. Every team who spent time there seemed to have at least one player who had some run-in.

Since then, others have lived through odd occurrences in the hotel. One player experienced an unpacking of his clothes and confirmed it was no one on the staff. Others have had objects in their rooms moved, have heard weird bangs and knocks, and have had doors open and close by unseen hands. The elevators start and stop on their own, and other electrical devices turn on and off or act weirdly.

"It's amazing how many people sleep with the lights on at the Vinoy," says Gordon. "It's kind of a new variation of the Motel 6 motto, 'We'll leave the lights on for you.'" The hotel is legendary throughout Major League Baseball. We kept having to revise our chapter, because every MLB clubhouse we visited added to the body of stories."

The most common story involves seeing a ghost. There are at least two spirits who make themselves known. The first is the younger man seen by Williamson and other players. Some feel he might be Benjamin Williamson, one of the original owners. There also is a lady in white who has been seen wafting through the halls, most often on the fifth floor. She is thought to be the ghost of another former owner, and the rumors are she was killed on the premises.

CHAPTER 7

WE'RE NOT ALONE ON THE WEST COAST

The West Coast is a microcosm of the country, a glimpse at what America is about and what it has to offer. It was forged by the pioneering spirit responsible for our very founding, and that spirit is still alive today. It has the major cities and industrial centers of the East Coast and the agricultural connections of the Midwest and Great Lakes region. It has the spirituality and sprawling mansions of the South. It also has all the phantoms seen in other states, with the traditions and ideas of Canada and Mexico finding their place in the reports of haunted places. Unlike some other parts of the country, the public eye is bright on the West Coast, even for those stories that struggle to see the light of day.

Tag, You're It

SALEM, OREGON

Ghosts can make themselves known anywhere at any time. The only hard rule when dealing with the paranormal is that there are no rules. That abandoned house down the street that just has to be haunted is silent, and that new condominium next door has been experiencing activity. The stereotypes have to be thrown out the window. For a real ghost story, forget what you see on television.

When you hear there is a ghost in Salem, it does not raise too much attention. Salem, Massachusetts, is known as the witch capital of the United States, and stories of phantoms are as common as corrupt politicians. The trouble is, this ghost was seen thousands of miles away in Salem, Oregon. Known as the Cherry City, the area is infamous for its Bigfoot sightings.

Henry does not grow cherries, and despite the woods surrounding his house, he has never seen a Bigfoot. In fact, his ghosts have very small feet. That might be due to the fact that Henry sees three children playing in his field, and one of them has no feet at all.

Henry enjoys his farm, although he has not grown anything more than some flowers on it in the twelve years he has lived there. Unlike many of his neighbors, he is retired, and his farm is still. After a lifetime in middle management, he settled down in his dream house overlooking several acres of pasture and woods and spends most days walking the field with his dog and painting pictures of the land he earned through hard work.

"It's the way it's supposed to be. You work and send the kids to college, and then you get to do nothing. That's my life. It'd be pretty boring if those kids didn't come around. My wife hasn't seen them, and I think she thinks I make them up, but there is a part of her who believes in ghosts," he says.

She should. Shortly after she and Henry moved into the house, their children threw the couple a party, setting them up with all of the necessities a retired couple needs. Among the gifts was a computer and lessons on how to use it. "I knew how it worked," says Henry. "I had used them before, and I like to think I was good for an old-timer. But Sam can't get the hang of it."

It was her confusion that led to the first sighting in the house. She had demanded that he leave the house so she could learn how to use the computer without him leaning over her. She was alone in the house, staring at the screen, when she saw a movement behind her in the monitor. She turned around but saw nothing. She could hear a woman humming, though, and followed the sound out of the room. She went back into the living room, confused about what she had seen and heard, and saw a woman standing over the computer. "She said the woman was wearing a long brown-and-white dress and had black hair done up in a bun. She was running her hand over the keyboard, but her hand was going through it. It was like she was trying to figure out what the computer was for," Henry says. The ghost, who appeared solid, turned and offered Sam a weak smile. She then quickly faded away.

"It took her a week to tell me. I have always believed in ghosts, so I took what she said as truth. She wasn't scared, or so she said. I could see she was upset, and I tried to make her laugh by saying a ghost knew more about e-mail than she did. It took a while, but she came to terms with what she had seen."

In a way, she was forced to. Although she has never seen anything else at the house, she has heard the footsteps that wake the couple up at night. "They're loud, like stomping. Like someone wearing heavy shoes tearing though the living room." Then there are locked doors that unlock by themselves. It happens a few times a year, and never when they are in the room. They lock a door, usually before going to sleep, and when they wake up, the door is unlocked and some-times open.

"Take it all in stride. That's my attitude about the whole thing. We don't tell anybody about it. It's too weird, and in a way it's like our own private thing."

What Henry really enjoys is waiting for the ghosts who run in his field. After seven years of hearing foot-steps and the occasional child's giggle, he finally saw a ghost for himself. "I was sitting on the back porch, and the sun was setting. I'd have to say, I was completely relaxed and enjoying the time. I saw a small boy, prob-ably about ten years old. He was wearing jeans and a white T-shirt and was walking just along the tree line of my yard. I had gotten to know most of the families in the neighborhood, and I didn't recognize him. I called out, and he turned and waved. Then he started to walk toward me. I noticed he didn't have any feet. His legs cut off just below the knee, and as he came toward me, he faded away. By the time he should have been about fifty feet from me, he was gone. I went out and walked that whole side of the yard. He was nowhere."

Henry told his wife what had happened, in part to get a rise out of her and partly to see if she had ever seen the boy. She did not quite believe him, and said she had never seen anybody other than the woman at the computer. The two did not seem to fit. The woman at the computer had seemed to be from an older time, but the boy had seemed modern.

Nothing else happened for a few months, and then the boy came back. "He was in the trees this time. It was the same time of day, but it was darker. I heard a whistling, like something you do when you're bored or not thinking. I followed the sound and saw him in the trees. He wasn't looking at me, but he was in a high branch, swinging his leg." Henry says the boy was wearing the same clothes and vanished completely as he approached.

"He was there, and then he was gone. He just puffed out, but without the smoke or anything. That was the second time, and I started to see him more after that." He would see the boy, whom he started to call Phil, about once a month, although he would sometimes see him twice a week if the mood was right. He was always near the tree line, and Henry got to walking it at sunset, taking his dog and asking Phil if he needed anything. The ghost never responded, but every once in a while, Henry would see him, always from a distance and always without feet.

"We had that kind of relationship for two years. Then he must have gotten bored with me. I was having my morning coffee one day, and I saw him. It was the first time I had ever seen him in the morning, and he wasn't looking at me." Instead, Henry says, the boy was looking behind him at two young girls, one about twelve and the other much younger, maybe five, who trailed behind her. They seemed to be running after Phil, and he would slow down just enough so they would almost catch him, and then he would speed up again.

"He was playing with them. Phil's my ghost, and he kinda has my personality. He was playing with them, and all three of them were laughing. They ran across the field, and when he was about ten yards from the trees, he faded and they faded with him. They never caught him."

The elderly man saw the three together only that one time, although he has seen Phil at least ten times since then. The encounters are confusing. The game of tag feels more like a residual haunting, but on most occasions, Phil recognizes Henry and waves to him. Perhaps the old farm is the scene of more than one type of haunting.

Henry is against trying to explain the phantoms on his farm, claiming he will never research the history of his house. "I don't need to. I know what I see, and I know what I hear. I don't need to know this kid died here or his name is Joe or something. It's perfect the way it is, and I see him just enough to make me know he's real and remind me there is something bigger out there."

Uncle Webb's Tools

LAKEWOOD, WASHINGTON

The haunted heart of the Pacific Northwest is the area of Washington around Seattle and Tacoma. There are too many haunted locations there to see in one day. People have met with tragedy because of the seafaring nature of its early settlement, and the influx of wealthy people has fostered interest in their eccentric lives and deaths. Whatever the reason, the ghost stories coming from that part of the country are numerous in their number and in the variety of the phantoms.

The crown jewel may be the Thornewood Castle Inn and Gardens located in Lakewood, Washington. The daunting 27,000-square-foot mansion has been the subject of haunted literature and rumor since it was built in the late nineteenth century. Hollywood decided the estate was worth filming and cast it as Rose Red in Stephen King's horror movie of the same name, and then recast it in the sequel, *The Diary of Ellen Rimbaur*. The hauntings there go beyond just the aesthetic. Chester Thorne, the man who built the house, has been seen in the halls and on the grounds outside. His son-in-law, who committed suicide on the property, has also made appearances.

Carl's house, a few miles away from the mansion, is much more humble but no less haunted. He has lived there for five years and has shared his house with at least two ghosts. One, whom he has nicknamed Kay, is a small girl who has a crush on him. While Carl was dating the woman who is now his wife, Kay would lock the doors when she would come over and pull the sheets off the couple.

Most of her activity revolves around an old music box he keeps in his dining room with his family's china. Kay has been known to move the box and place it in other rooms. She also winds it with invisible hands and can be heard humming along with the music.

"It plays 'Raindrops Keep Falling on My Head,' but she likes the old song. I keep it around just because it belonged to my mother, who died. I hear it all the time, or it's in my kitchen on the counter. I put it back, but the dust in the cabinet isn't moved," Carl says.

Kay might be playful, but Carl and his wife have learned to live with her. "She's gotten used to my wife and just wants to play. I have no trouble with her."

The same could not be said for his Uncle Webb, who spent a few months in the house after his death from cancer in 2005. "I don't know if there is something with the house, but I think we drew him in. He didn't like me having those tools."

Webb's first name was Charlie, but with so many relatives with that name, he decided to go by his middle name. He was a contractor, who always hoped his son, Jimmy, would follow in his footsteps. Jimmy went to college to become a teacher, and although he originally put up a fight about it, Webb eventually broke down and embraced his son's decision. "He wanted Jimmy to be a contractor, but to be honest, Jimmy was all thumbs. He couldn't even hang a picture."

After graduating from college, Carl went on to become a computer programmer but understood the need to be useful around the house. After his uncle's death, his aunt gave him all of Webb's tools, knowing he would put them to good use.

"It started two weeks after the funeral. I had set up a little work area in the basement and put all the tools down there. One night I was in bed, tired after a long day in front of a monitor, and I heard a crash downstairs. I went into the basement and all the tools were scattered around. I'm an odd person. I put everything in the right place and I know I hung all those tools up and organized everything down there," Carl says.

He went back to bed, shaking his head, and did not get around to putting the tools away that weekend. When he observed the mess that Saturday morning, he noticed none of the hooks that held the tools were

bent and that they were thrown throughout the basement in places they could not have gotten to naturally.
"A hammer was under an old desk I have down there.
For it to have gotten there, someone would have had
to throw it. It's a good ten feet away."

A few days later, his wife was washing dishes when
she noticed that a picture had fallen off the wall. "It
was on the kitchen table. I didn't put it there, and my
wife had nothing to do with it." The glass of the picture, which showed his wife during her trip to Europe,
was shattered. "There was a screwdriver right through
the glass. It was like someone had tried to stab her in
the picture."

His wife was frightened by the incident, even
though the family had experience with the paranormal. "I know there are people in my house. This felt
differently and we were trying to figure out who it
might be."

They got their answer in the next few days. "Uncle
Webb had always liked the Beatles. Radios in our house
started to turn on and play Beatles songs. I mean, we
have a radio in just about every room in the house.
They would turn on by themselves, and a Beatles song
would play. They'd be on stations neither of us even
listens to. I began to wonder if it was Uncle Webb and
what he wanted."

The couple decided it was just him trying to communicate that he had moved on. Tools continued to
be moved, and radios continued to play. After three

weeks, they were beginning to get tired of moving around the house turning off stereos. "I asked him to tell me what was wrong. If he had something to say, I asked him to say it. I didn't really think I would get a response."

That night, all of the radios in the house turned on, all playing the same song. Carl turned them all off one by one and moved to the basement to shut the last one off.

"There it was. All of the tools were in a perfect circle on the floor of the basement. In the middle was a picture of my cousin Jimmy and me. That picture had been in the attic in a box of pictures. There is no way it could have gotten into the basement.

"I figured he wanted Jimmy to have the tools. I packed them up the next day and drove to Seattle where he lives. I didn't tell him what happened. I just gave him the box and told him they belong to him. He was actually kind of happy about it. I'm not sure if he ever uses them, but they're his now."

Carl says the music has since stopped, and all of the pictures in his house stay where they are supposed to be.

The Haunted Neighborhood

Seattle's Capitol Hill is home to two of the most active cemeteries in the area: the Grand Army of the Republic Cemetery and Lake View Cemetery. Both are frequented by the living because of the famous people buried there and the reports of ghosts. People often find the time to visit both on a trip to the city.

The Grand Army of the Republic Cemetery is home to many of the soldiers who fought in the Civil War. Their ghosts have been seen roaming the rows at night, and gunshots have been heard coming from the middle. Lights are the most common sighting, but some people have seen the soldiers in full dress, and several have seen the ghosts during the day. It is unclear why these ghosts would be seen, although many of the graves have been moved over the years, perhaps keeping the spirits from finding peace.

Lakeview boasts several famous graves, many of which have strong haunted lore attached to them. In one of the most touching and disturbing turns in the paranormal world, the ghosts of both martial arts actor Bruce Lee and his son, movie star Brandon Lee, are seen in the same cemetery. The two are never seen together, but on separate instances they have been spotted during the day and at night. The elder is seen sitting at his own grave, sometimes sitting on a nearby bench, or sitting in front in a praying position. Brandon has more of a habit of wandering near the headstones and then straying to walk to other plots. Both have been seen as full apparitions, and both have been known to disappear or dissolve when people try to get their attention. Perhaps both could find rest if they could see each other.

The Battle

SACRAMENTO, CALIFORNIA

People react differently when they touch the paranormal. Many fall back on silence, the best defense mechanism. They say to themselves, "Nothing ever happened." When the activity intensifies, people find that they can no longer hide, and they have to confront the unknown head on. Many turn to local paranormal investigators, especially in this day and age when one can be found with a quick search on the Internet. Many still fall back on the traditional method. They turn to their faith and their church. Whether it is the power of the members or the source they call upon, or just the intention of the people involved, this can often get results. Sometimes, however, it comes back to haunt them.

Connie moved into her house the day before Halloween in 2004. She had recently made the move to Sacramento from San Diego and was happy to have a place for her and her son, Josh, after having lived in a hotel while the house was in escrow. The house in Sacramento was bigger than she could have dreamed. It was 1,765 square feet with four bedrooms and three full baths, maybe too big for the two of them but better than they had before. Soon the house would become too small for them and their uninvited guests.

"The first night we spent in the house was kind of eerie feeling. We slept downstairs, in the living room. We didn't have anything in the house but clothes, blankets, and pillows. I woke up to a mild knock on the wall by the master bedroom upstairs. I got up and asked myself, 'What is that?' The knocking continued from 1:00 A.M. to 3:00 A.M. I told myself it was probably just the wood creaking," she says.

She called the Realtor, who told her it was only the pipes and shifting wood caused by the empty house getting heat now that it had new tenants. The response seemed reasonable, but the noises continued. "Every night, I was experiencing this knock on the wall, but I continued to ignore it."

The noise did not stop when they moved upstairs and settled into the house. "I was awoken by the mild knock one morning at 1:00 A.M. I had to go and use the bathroom, so I got up and went and the knock followed me. It knocked multiple times behind me, and I got up and started to open up the boxes to search for my Bible. I started praying in Jesus's name, saying, 'I rebuke the spirit in this house that doesn't belong here. Follow the light and leave.' I read Psalm 23, Psalm 119, and Psalm 91 loudly. Each night, I found myself doing the same routine, and whatever it was would stop."

Connie had already missed too much work and had to hire a nanny. The nanny was a seventy-three-year-old Filipino woman, but the hire proved to cause tension. The woman claimed that she was in touch with the dead and could see people in the house. She claimed there were spirits in her bedroom that removed her blankets and blew air on her feet. They would whisper in her ears and giggle. Connie told her she was imagining things. Part of her did not believe the stories, but the larger reason was that she had to work to pay for the house. She did not have time to deal with it. Ghosts have a habit of forcing people to notice them and make the time.

"One evening, the nanny called me crying, saying they were messing with the garage door, moving it up and down repeatedly. She said she had tried to call me, but the phone had no dial tone. I had to go home and check on her to see if she was all right. When I got home, the garage door was wide open. I knew I left it shut.

"I was beginning to question if the nanny was insane. I told her to calm down, that everything was going to be okay. Each night, these things happened. It was affecting my job. Then, finally, she quit. She told me to move out of the house before someone got hurt. She told me she saw a woman coming out of the master bedroom and going into her room, but she never came out."

The next week, Connie hired a man who was not intimidated by the activity in the house. Things were normal for a while, but a friend had an experience that forced Connie to confront what was in the house.

"When I got home one day, I found a home-cooked meal my coworker had left at the door. The house alarm was just going crazy. My phone was ringing, but I was just too busy trying to open the door, and I ignored it.

I got in the house, situated my sleeping three-year-old in bed, and went downstairs to deactivate the alarm. I finally answered the phone, and it was my coworker who had brought me the dinner. She said, 'Get out of there. Get your baby and get out!' I grabbed my son, ran out the door, and got into my van."

Connie's neighbors stopped her and told her no one ever stayed in the house for long. Recently, people had lived in the house for only months at a time. Connie was starting to get nervous and began putting the pieces together. When she arrived at her friend's house, she heard more evidence. "My friend said she was knocking and she saw someone peek through the blinds upstairs. Then she heard someone coming down the stairs and waited for someone to open the door. No one was there. She felt goose bumps all over. She left the food at the door and took off."

Connie contacted her local church. The whole church came to the house and anointed the house with oil, said prayers, and sang gospel songs. The method was so effective that they decided to have a weekly Bible study to keep the forces in the house at bay.

It wasn't quiet for long. Connie received a call at work from her nanny, who claimed something was opening and closing the bedroom doors. "The new nanny told me that something shut the door in his room as he was putting Josh to sleep. A child called for Josh to come into the other room and told him to close the door and don't let the nanny in." The nanny grabbed Josh and took him into his room. "He asked

Josh who called him into that room. 'Billy wants me to stay with him in the room and play!'"

The nanny asked for permission to quit. He told her he was scared and did not want anything to happen to her son and get blamed for it. Connie rented an apartment to soothe him and to think things out for herself. She only went back to the house to do yard work and laundry. If they had to go into the house, she would pray and make sure to take her Bible. "Each time I did this, I would hear a sound of running people from downstairs to upstairs as if they were running away."

Whatever was in the house began reaching out to members of the church. "Once, a spirit called one of the church member's cell phone and left a message on his voice mail. The message sounded so evil. A growly voice said, 'This house belongs to me.'"

The final episode happened in the summer of 2005. "I was cooking dinner in preparation for Bible study. My friend Winnie, who was about seven months pregnant, was visiting me. As I was cooking dinner, I was telling her a story about someone from work who had literally robbed me. As I was discussing this greedy person, I got upset and started cursing. As I was cursing, a sudden loud smack on the wall by the kitchen cabinet suddenly shocked us. It was so loud; it sounded like a hand was smacking the wall about six times."

Connie was scared by the noise, but her friend Winnie was so frightened that she thought she was going to have her baby. Connie had had enough. It was time to move out.

That was the deciding point. It all became too much. "I finally moved out. I rented the house to other people, but no one stayed very long. They never did say why. We're now residing in San Diego and have no plans to go anywhere." Today, she feels the move to Sacramento brought out something dark in her because she had split up her family and moved there for the wrong reasons, including revenge for something that had happened to her. The haunting and the insight she gained from the fight with what was in her house were God's way of telling her to let go of the bad things in her life.

"I know the ending of the story doesn't sound like a ghost story. But ghosts are the biggest fear I have, so God used it to straighten up my act." She never saw the people her nannies did, but knew there was something dark there. Some ghost stories are like a circle. The spirit is identified, and the family finds a balance. Connie might have a reason for her haunting, but she still cannot fully understand what was in her house. Instead of reasons, she has an empty dream house and a stronger faith.

Great-Grandpa

ANAHEIM, CALIFORNIA

Anaheim is the land of fantasy. A half-hour outside Los Angeles and the home of Disneyland, it is a town based in the unreal and submerged in dreams. The town is about the sizzle and survives on spinning the package. It does its job well, and the illusion becomes the reality. Mixing the two is big business, and finding the balance becomes a full-time job. Even its name is a made-up word combining the tradition of the area and the German heritage it was founded on. Among the rides and amusements that make up the personality of the city, you will find many tributes to the paranormal, but for Anaheim, ghosts are part of the story, not the reality.

Bernie had a relationship with her great-grandfather, but some might say it was more like a dream. She spent her childhood and teen years seeing him and spending time getting to know the man. The trouble was, he killed himself in the family house a year before she was born.

"The first experience I can recall would have been about 1982 or 1983. I was in the family house, which belonged to my great-grandmother at that time. She was a night owl and restless, so it wasn't uncommon for me to wake up in her room in the middle of the night to hear her puttering around the house.

"One night, I woke up to the sound of her doing dishes in the kitchen. I had the feeling that I was not alone in her bedroom. I looked over to the bedroom door and could see a man standing there watching me sleep. It bothered me a little, but when I realized I could see though him to the wall on the opposite side, I figured I was dreaming and closed my eyes again."

She never mentioned the incident and assumed it was all a trick of her eyes. A few years later, the man made himself known again. "I was again dozing in my great-grandmother's bed when I felt something brush my cheek, like a kiss. I could hear her wood floor creaking under the weight of someone's feet. I sat up in bed to ask my great-grandmother if I could get up and sit with her for a while. The man was again standing in the bedroom doorway, only this time he raised his hand to me in salutation and faded out."

Seeing the man this time was more disturbing, and she began to scream. Her great-grandmother came into the room and tried to comfort her. She described the man, and her great-grandmother left and came back with a box of old pictures. She stopped on one picture, and staring back at Bernie was the man she had seen. "The man in the hallway was her husband, my great-grandfather. I was later told that I had said several times as a small child there was a man lying in the hallway covered in blood and begging for someone to help him."

Realizing the man was related to her seemed to have triggered more activity in the house, although there was more than one ghost living with the family. "It became commonplace to hear footsteps in the hallway at all hours or for the toilet to flush when no one was in the bathroom. The end of the hallway, the spot where he had been found after his suicide, was always colder than the surrounding air, no matter the time of year. Small items around the house would go missing when they had been laid in plain sight—house and car keys, money, jewelry, homework, shopping lists. We would take the house nearly apart looking for them, and they would be nowhere to be found. We would have to ask politely to have the item back. When we would return to the room, the missing item would be sitting in the middle of a table as if it had been there all along. I felt watched everywhere I went."

Bernie was not the only person who experienced the haunting, and it became harder to hide the activity in the house. "People sleeping in the house would feel the blankets moved on beds as they slept, or a hand tickling them. Doors would slam on days there was no wind at all, and we would hear stomping footsteps through the house. The television would change channels or turn off unexpectedly, and lights flickered constantly."

There was protection for Bernie, though. Her great-grandmother had a measure of control over her husband. "When I became frightened, she would stalk out to the living room or hallway, a wooden spoon in one hand that she shook at the air as she scolded him for his jokes as if he were alive and standing in front of her. After each scolding, the house would be quiet for a few months before the pranks would start up again."

Things changed when Bernie was fifteen. Her great-grandmother grew ill and had to be hospitalized. Bernie was sick herself, and the doctors would not let her visit. The illness also meant she had to sleep on the couch in the living room so it would be easier for her to get her medicine and entertain herself during the sleepless hours. Her grandmother stayed with her while her mother was often away watching over her great-grandmother.

"It was late one night in February that I woke up to the feeling of someone sitting on the side of my bed and a cool hand brushing my face. The bed creaked and dipped under the weight, and I rolled over to face it, expecting to see my nana sitting there to check on me. There was no one sitting there. I looked down and could see the bed curved as if someone was sitting there and the tension on the blanket as it pulled from the weight. My nana was asleep in a recliner not five feet away. I knew my mother was still at work because I had not heard her come in.

"Very quietly, I asked if my great-grandfather was there with me. At the foot of my bed sat a music box. It was not wound up, but it began to play. It played for about nine or ten notes, more than it would have played if it simply had some tension left, and stopped. I felt something brush my forehead again. This time it reminded me of a kiss on the forehead. Then the bed relaxed and sprang back into place."

The nighttime kiss became a regular thing, and although the people in the house knew there was a ghost present, they did not believe her great-grandfather was visiting her at night. They thought the sickness was making her see things. Her great-grandmother got worse as Bernie got better, and eventually she was well enough to say her goodbyes. Bernie was excited to see her loved one again, and something wanted her to go, as well.

"We were getting ready when my mother walked into the kitchen to get a drink of water. When she turned around, she tripped over a chair that was pulled out from the kitchen table. She reminded me I needed to push the kitchen chairs in when I was done. I had not been in the kitchen that morning at all. I got up to protest my innocence and walked in just as the cabinet door swung open and nearly hit my mother in the back of the head.

"As my mother closed the cabinet doors again, the chair she had just pushed in pulled away from the table by itself and hit her in the knees. She yelled at me as she turned around but immediately went pale when she saw I was all the way across the room and obviously not able to have pushed the chair.

"She pushed the chair in, and the cabinet swung open again. It went on like that for several minutes— cabinets reopening, chairs sliding across the floor, the front and back door slamming open and shut, stomping footfalls through the house in a very clear pattern from front door to back door.

"We both began to cry. My mother was trapped in the kitchen because every time she moved, something in the kitchen moved to intercept her. She started to scream and beg him to stop, reminding him of who she was. As suddenly as it began, it stopped. The house felt like it was in a vacuum. Not that the temperature had changed, but it was silent. Always before, there was a sense of life to the house; now it felt absent and empty. My mother and I looked at each other in horror, then at the clock. We both felt something was horribly wrong. We grabbed our purses and ran out the door. Whatever had occurred, we both felt an immediate and urgent need to be at the hospital. When we arrived, the doctor met us in the hallway to tell us my great-grandmother had passed. When my mother asked when, the time of death was the exact time that our house had fallen completely silent."

Although they were both frightened by the incident in the kitchen, Bernie feels it was her great-grandfather trying to force them to leave and get to the hospital quickly. And she thinks that he was angry his wife was passing. She never saw her great-grandfather again but remembers him fondly now. All of the things she experienced were frightening if taken by themselves, but it was a relationship she otherwise never would have had with the man. She did not get to see her great-grandmother before she died, but her great-grandfather made that easier.

I'm Still with You

LOS ANGELES AND SAN DIEGO, CALIFORNIA

The paranormal often gets pushed aside as mere coincidence. When things happen, we rationalize the supernatural, giving reasons why a radio turned on when it should not have or why a set of keys, always placed on the hook, suddenly appears on the nightstand. Alone, these happenings can be explained away, but when they begin to stack up, it becomes harder and harder to deny something may be trying to make contact. Keep ignoring it, keeping trying to push out the unseen, and it might just push back. When all logical explanations are exhausted, it is time to look to the paranormal and see something behind those little signs dropped into your life for a reason you cannot understand. When the ghost is your relative, like your sister whose life was cut short, the messages can be comforting if you can translate them.

Pamela was a believer in the paranormal but had never had an experience until 2002. That year, her younger sister, only thirty-five years old, died suddenly from an aneurism. The quick, unexplained nature of the death bewildered and saddened everyone, but Pamela would not spend too much time without her beloved sibling. Only a few months later, her sister made contact, comforting and confusing her at the same time. It took a while to convince Pamela that she was making contact with a ghost, but now her mind is set that her sister had something to say.

"One night, I awoke in the middle of the night to go to the bathroom and noticed that the stereo was on in my living room," she says. "I didn't think much of it. I just turned it off and went back to bed. A few nights later, I got up and again the stereo was on. I thought I must have pressed a wrong button on the stereo, which made the timer come on or something." The stereo continued to turn on in the night, at least a dozen times in the first few months. With each new occurrence, she found a new excuse as to why it had happened. There was nothing in the songs playing or the time the radio would turn on to suggest anything out of the ordinary. It was just a bad stereo or a bad wire somewhere.

The message trying to get through found a way to refine itself. "One afternoon, I went to a garage sale and bought an oil painting of angels and brought it home. I was up on a chair hanging it when my stereo clicked on, in the middle of the day, all by itself, and started playing a song in my five-disc CD player." She had gotten used to the unexplained music, but this song was one about angels; it was one of her favorites. The music rang through the house, much louder than she ever normally turned her radio up, and she began to feel someone was there.

The messages continued one day in her car. She had pulled her car over and was searching all over the seats and glove compartment for something she had lost when the radio turned on by itself and played another popular song about angels. "No way that could have happened. But the message was so calming that it did make me feel better when I was so upset," she says.

Someone else soon witnessed the weird experiences. She and her boyfriend were talking one day as she walked back and forth in front of the television. It turned on by itself in front of both of them. She was glad to have a witness to what had been happening to her, and it happened several more times to them in the next few months. Pamela began to believe it was a ghost, and her mind naturally went to her sister. It had all begun after she had died, and the meanings behind many of the songs were comforting and helpful, just the kind of thing her sister would do. She now admits that she was not completely sold on the idea at that time.

The spirit was not confined to her house. In addition to making itself known in different places, it also traveled with her to her new apartment. Before she left her old home, the spirit had another message for her. "All my stuff had been put in storage except for a futon and a small boom box that had an old CD in it. When I got home from storing my stuff that day and walked back into my home for my last night, the boom box was on all by itself again." The radio played a popular song about leaving, and Pamela broke down. "I just cried and cried sitting there on the floor in my empty home, hearing these words sing to me. It was the most eerie feeling. I still never really thought it was a ghost. I didn't know what to think, really. Just knew there was something out there that knew me and was trying to communicate with me."

Things did not change when she moved to San Diego. The television in the bedroom continued to turn on and off, even though she plugged it into different outlets and rearranged the room, and the stereo kept playing by itself. "I would wake up in the middle of the night to go to the bathroom, and I would walk into the hall and my stereo would come on. It was starting to drive me a little nuts. I would go over to turn it down, and it would just turn louder, and I would have to pull out the plug to make it stop. It was freaky. I had a bootleg CD, and it had bad static on it. I awoke, and the static was playing in the middle of the night. I went to turn it down, and it turned louder. It would not turn down. It was so strange and happened so much that I finally just gave that stereo away."

The trouble was not the stereo. Something was still trying to be heard. "About a month after I gave it away the strangest thing happened. I had loud neighbors who lived in the unit under me, and one night, at about two in the morning, the stereo in the bedroom below me came on. I was so angry, I got up and stormed into my hallway. The hall light came on all by itself. Then I went downstairs and knocked on my neighbors' door to tell them to shut off the music. Much to my surprise, no one was home."

In the three years since her sister's death, Pamela believes her sister has made contact with her at least twenty times, always through some electrical device. She has been in different settings with different televisions and radios. Once, her sister even used the computer. It happens at random times, although she can count on it happening when she is having a hard time emotionally. Sometimes the ghost is helpful, like when it seemed to find her lost earrings. Sometimes it is profound, like when it plays certain songs that fit the situation Pamela is in. Usually, her sister just seems to want to say hello.

Then there is the time the spirit helped change her life. "I had gone out that day to buy some pot from someone, and when I came in my home that evening, the stereo was playing," Pamela says. The song was about losing oneself for other people. The meaning seemed clear to her. Although she was not a heavy drug user, marijuana had been interfering with her life and her relationships. "I have never forgotten that. It made me stop buying pot. That was years ago."

It is hard for Pamela to make sense of it all. She is open-minded, but the pieces do not fit together. She is sure the ghost is her sister, even today, as she continues to get communications. Although, she is not sure why she is the only one in her family to make contact. It would be easier if she heard her sister's voice or received some more specific clue to her sister's life. "All the songs—it is from the spirit world. They can get messages through to us, even if it's just to calm us down when we are upset, or letting us know they feel our pain when we are leaving and don't know where we are going. We definitely get messages from the other side.

"Playful little poltergeist my sister is. It's got to be her on the other side communicating with me. Things like this never happened before she died. Wish I knew how to communicate back with her. It used to really scare me. Now I am just used to it, and almost wish I knew what to do. It's like someone's trying to reach out to me, but I don't know how to reach back." Sometimes the thing to do is just listen and try not to understand.

CHAPTER 8

GHOSTS MAKE AN APPEARANCE IN THE MIDWEST AND GREAT LAKES REGION

The Midwest and the Great Lakes region are the backbone of our country. People are grounded realists, not quick to jump at superstitions, but they also have one foot planted in the other side. Maybe there is something about the flat land and the distant horizons in the Midwest, but there have been haunted reports from all over the heartland, starting at the major cites of different states and spreading out to the quieter, rural areas. The rest of the United States might see this part of the country as calm and demure, the average America that products and television cater to. There is no average haunting, and the experiences there are just as gripping, just as outside the norm, as anything seen from one coast to the other.

Just Another Haunting

CHERRY VALLEY, ILLINOIS

Sometimes we have to ask what a haunting is. We can give definitions and explanations, but coming up with a real answer is difficult. Hauntings are as varied as the people who experience them, which clouds the understanding as to just what they are. Some ghosts haunt a place. People with no interest or desire experience something they cannot explain. Sometimes ghosts appear to the same person over and over again. It is said that once you open yourself up to them, more ghosts will find you. You become a beacon of light as they travel through darkness, and they will go after anyone who is willing to talk. In Cherry Valley, the townspeople know about several haunted places. Jessica's story was a bit more personal.

Jessica does not consider herself to be psychic or more sensitive to the paranormal than the people around her. People who do not know her all that well say she has an overactive imagination, but those who are closest to her know she does not make up stories. The stories come to her. She has been seeing ghosts since she was young, and she and her family have seen the supernatural to the point that it has become commonplace. Some ghosts are not always pleasant. "While I was growing up, ghosts, spirits, or whatever they may be loved to pick on me," she says.

She admits she was an odd little kid, and she learned very early on that there might be something else out there. "My first experience was at the age of four. I can remember sitting in the bathroom when suddenly my toy bus very slowly came from my bedroom across the hallway into the bathroom. Now most children would have screamed and run for their mothers. I, however, from what I remember, just looked at the toy and laughed. I was a strange child."

Jessica's grandmother's house had a long and colorful history before their family even moved in. It had been built in the 1880s, possibly even earlier than that, and was a dance hall. The land it is on was once a park for the town of Cherry Valley, an area with more than just a passing knowledge of ghosts. "My grandmother's house was supposedly haunted. They bought the house in the late 1930s and began adding onto it in the 1950s. Until then, the house had been quiet."

Often a haunting begins with changes made to a house. One idea is that the energy change sparks a ghost that is already there and makes it easier to see. The more accepted belief is that the change interrupts the safe place the ghost knows. Imagine people moving into your house and making it their own. You would be helpless to stop them and angry.

The family knew about the ghost, and Jessica became acquainted with it when she would visit. "Playing in my grandmother's room, I would often hear footsteps coming down the stairs when the only other person in the house was in the kitchen. It never frightened me, but it drove me crazy because I could never get there fast enough to see what was coming down the stairs."

There might have been something about the house or the land it was on that attracted ghosts. Some places are more haunted than others, and some of the old residents have no reason to remain. Years after her first experiences, there was a new presence in the house. "My grandfather died in 1977, and it was shortly after that the rocking chair by the bed I slept in would rock by itself. I would wake up in the middle of the night hearing someone walk across the floor and then hear the chair rock. I would sit up in bed and it would stop. Numerous times I got up to check windows to see what was making the chair move. I never found anything."

The things happening in the house did not frighten Jessica. She was not intimidated, especially by her grandfather. There was one part of the house she could not deal with, though, and whatever was there was not like the energy in the rest of the house. "Only one part of the house truly terrified me, and it was an odd spot. The top of the second-floor stairs would send a chill down my spine. I dreaded walking up those stairs as a child and would run as fast as I could to the playroom or bedroom. I always felt safe in those rooms. Years later, talking to my mother about the house, we both confided in each other how that landing put such fear in both of us." Off the landing was a room that was kept locked, although Jessica does not remember why.

"One night, my cousin and I both awoke to a light glowing from the room that was always locked. I was fascinated, but my poor cousin never slept upstairs again."

Her grandmother eventually sold the property, and Jessica went on to have experiences in other places. Perhaps it was the random nature of the haunting or the fact that she was never able to trace what was happening, but there is something that will always draw her back to the house.

Haunted Bloods Point Road

Bloods Point Road in Farmerville, Illinois, the next-door neighbor of Cherry Valley, is a place where ghosts and legends walk together. The stretch of road claims to be the home of at least two specters in a nearby cemetery and a haunted bridge. The bridge is the haunting ground of the ghosts of little children who were in a bus accident on the bridge. In addition to witnessing little giggles and ghost lights, a driver can park on the bridge, put the car in neutral, and have something unseen push the car across the bridge. The bridge is also the sight of a witch hanging, and her ghost haunts it and an abandoned house in the neighborhood. Of course, there are also rumors of a mother who killed her children and cursed her house. The children got their revenge a year later by scaring her to death.

The backstory is rumor and legend, but the experiences are true. Bloods Point Road has been the spot of genuine ghosts. People have seen little children who giggle and disappear in the cemetery there at night. People have reported seeing lights on in houses that are supposed to be empty. Black figures walk the side of the road and appear and disappear at will. The stretch of road is a great place for paranormal investigators and legend trippers alike.

The Prank

VANDALIA, ILLINOIS

Small towns are filled with ghosts, although it is difficult at times to crack the personality of a place and get to the tale. Cities often publicize the phantoms of their towns, especially if they are connected with a business. People share stories on message boards and encourage others to go to the same places and see what they can find. Small towns are different. They keep their stories secret and clam up to outsiders. When strangers find their way to towns like Vandalia, Illinois, they find out that the town secrets hold something more than just history. They often hold ghosts.

In the world of the paranormal, there is a thing known as a time slip, in which the witness is temporarily taken out of the present and sees a moment of the past. The witness cannot interact with the ghosts she sees, and the experience doesn't last long. People who experience time slips are left wondering why, and they often spend the rest of their lives trying to get people to believe them and understand why the time slips happened. Time slips are often associated with historic places, but secrets, like those kept in small towns, can stir them, as well.

Rob runs a paranormal radio show out of the Florida panhandle. He investigates the local ghost scene and talks to many people, on and off the air, in an attempt to understand what has happened to him in his life. He has had many paranormal experiences over the years, many of them during his childhood. One happened when he was about eleven years old and would have discouraged most people from ever seeing a horror movie again.

His father had just lost his job. He had been a decorated war hero, but his service had left scars on him that could not be seen but had a devastating effect on him and his family. "He often couldn't focus and was subject to night terrors," Rob says. "War has many casualties that survive it, I suppose, and it creates casualties off the front lines when they return. I'm proud of my father and what he did, but reality demands I be honest in that he often made our lives very difficult. Moving from place to place, and many times we were forced to stay with relatives in between his lost jobs."

The moving was difficult for the family, and eventually they found their way to the small town of Vandalia, Illinois. They lived far away from their neighbors, and the isolation did nothing to lift the family's spirits. There were ten children and four adults living in the house, including Rob's sister Brenda. He thought there was something dangerous in the house from the time they drove down the dirt road. His fears were quickly washed away when he found the pond behind it. There were turtles, snakes, frogs, and anything else a boy his age would need to keep himself occupied.

Despite having his own room in the large house, something made it difficult to settle in. "I never slept well, and from time to time, I thought I heard banging noises coming from around the one [uncurtained] window in the room. It led directly to the roof over the laundry room. I never looked out that window at night because it gave me that feeling I hated. I didn't quite know what it was back then, but I know it made me afraid, and I know it felt like someone else was there with me when I got it."

The family lived there for some time, squeaking out a living and becoming accustomed to the house. Often Rob would try to play with the older children, but they did their best to ditch him as they went out for their own adventures, usually picking wild berries to help feed the family. On one of these journeys, they found a shack. It was rundown and overgrown and known only by rumor. "A man had murdered his wife there, stabbing her multiple times while she sat at their upright piano. My cousins always made sure to tell me the history, though I had no interest to learn. It gave me that feeling.

"Once, my cousin decided to stay back and keep me company as the others had once again run far ahead, leaving me behind. I was grateful to have her there, as I didn't feel the need to run and catch up. It was always so hot, and the dust would stick to me, turning into mud upon my sweating skin. We were passing by the rundown old shack, as we had done a million times before, only this time she wanted to go in and look around. By this time, the other kids had gone out of sight, and I was alone with only her for comfort and companionship.

"As I walked on the property, pushing my way behind her through the thickets of overgrown weeds that towered well above my head, we came to the front door. It was half off its hinges, lying crooked in the frame. I felt an overwhelming panic course through my entire body. She prodded me to come on. I stood there, wanting to burst into tears and run away. I walked forward, and as I did, she pushed me through the door, laughing.

"I had fallen onto the wood floor just inside the house. My knees and hands hurt from the impact as I tried to catch myself. The door, which barely stood before, suddenly slammed shut with such force and so fast I don't remember having enough time to flinch. I could hear my cousin scream outside. The room sort of lit up with a dim light that wasn't coming from any-where. I got very cold. The sweat from the heat of day chilled me to the bone.

"I don't know how to describe it exactly. It was as if I were being pulled or held down by a great force. I felt as if I suddenly weighed hundreds of pounds, and I could barely keep my elbows from bending as I fought having my head touch the floor. I didn't want my face to touch that floor. I don't know why, but I couldn't let that happen. I could hear music from a piano, and I could smell food cooking and hear a man's voice. I couldn't make out what he was saying.

"In front of me was a living room with a round carpet in the center, a couch with two end tables on each side of it, and there was a woman sitting at a piano. She didn't even seem to see me. Then it went completely black again. It just all went away. I became aware of my cousin's screams outside, and she was crying now. The door opened back up, landing against the inside wall, and I could see her standing outside in the light. She was screaming for me to run outside to her. I could tell part of her wanted to grab me, but she couldn't bring herself to approach the door. I still couldn't move. The force, whatever it was, was still holding me. I began to cry, and as I did, I could hear a woman's voice. It was trying to comfort me and it said, 'Let him go.' It was then I felt the release and ran outside."

To this day, his cousin refuses to talk about what happened and leaves the room if asked. Just as he was alone that day in the shack, Rob is left alone to wonder.

The Passenger on the Bus

MINNEAPOLIS, MINNESOTA

The dead are all around us, asking to be heard and seen. They might have a reason to make contact, sometimes just for contact's sake, but their cries go unheard. Sometimes we make contact and do not know it until the moment is over. We are left with a feeling that something happened and usually feel that we would do something different if it happens again. Usually, we have one shot at it, and the moment is frozen in time, unexplained.

Jenny was a morning radio personality at the University of Minnesota in Minneapolis and would often take the bus into work. At that time of the morning, the bus carried a few students and commuters but was empty for the most part. She would usually be half-awake as she traveled when the winter mornings were really no different from the winter nights.

"It was 5:00 A.M., and the winter was very dark at this time," Jenny recalls. "I was listening to music on my headphones and looking out the window when I caught the reflection of a woman smiling at me. She was a white woman and had short dark hair. Her smile was pleasant enough." Jenny says there was nothing about the woman that made her think anything was odd, except for perhaps the smile that early in the morning. But when she turned, she realized something that was different about her friendly commuter.

"I turned to look across the aisle where it seemed she was sitting, but nobody was there. When I looked back at the window, she was still there smiling at me. Once more, I looked back at the seat across and still did not see her. There were only a few other people on the bus with me but not the woman I saw in the window. When I looked back at the window to see if she was still there, she was gone."

The sighting had a profound effect on Jenny, and she still carries it with her today. "I felt paralyzed and sick and remember that I had goose bumps all over. I was so disturbed I had to take my headphones off. Once in a while, I would carefully look around the bus to catch another glimpse of her, but I never saw her again. I held back tears the whole ride to school and cried a lot as soon as I got off the bus."

Years later, she remembers what the woman looked like and the way she felt. "I was pretty disturbed the rest of the day but had to carry on with my normal activities. Overall, I feel lucky I had such a life-changing experience that very few people get to encounter. When it first happened, I wondered if she was smiling at me because I reminded her of someone, but I do not know. I considered myself an atheist before the incident, but the experience made me unsure of a lot of things. I am not as scared of death or dying. My grandpa died about a week before I saw the ghost, so in a way, it made me feel better about his death."

Land of Ten Thousand Haunted Schools

Minnesota seems to have as many haunted schools as it does bodies of water. Duluth Central High School suffers the spirit of a young woman who was supposedly raped and then killed herself a short time later. Her cries are heard when other students are alone in the bathroom, and some have reported bloody fingerprints on the mirror and sink and her calling out the names of those who raped her. She also has been heard apologizing, although it is unclear as to what she is apologizing for. Duluth's East High School is haunted by a fallen director who interrupts productions. Students at Moorhead State University in Moorhead, Minnesota, have seen the legless ghost of an old employee who died on a set of stairs there after falling and breaking his neck and legs.

The most haunted campus may be at St. Cloud State University in St. Cloud, Minnesota. There, the hauntings are linked to scandal and rumor. At North Shoemaker Hall, the ghost of a cafeteria worker who committed suicide in the meat locker makes scratching sounds and locks and unlocks the storage room. Some say that the haunting is actually at Shoemaker Hall and that the worker was a student who had been having an affair with a janitor. She has also been reported to float over beds and move objects. In Lawrence Hall, the students have to deal with another employee gone bad. In the 1950s, a janitor killed two teachers. The building is not in use today, but people have seen lights turn on and off from the outside and a mysterious man who is reported to appear in windows.

Blue Men and Women in White

BATTLE CREEK, MICHIGAN

Paranormal researchers come across stories of children all the time. Although the tales can be easily dismissed, the young seem to have a vision the rest of us lose as we get older. Perhaps their minds are too innocent, and they have not been told that ghosts do not exist. They see because they have not been told not to see. Perhaps it has to do with the way the brain works. As we develop our higher reasoning, somehow it knocks out our ability to use the psychic side of our brains, closing our eyes to phantoms.

The reports come in all the time. Over a baby monitor, parents hear their children talking to someone, only to hear someone respond. Or they hear a child talking about a dead relative. Imaginary friends have shared knowledge kids would not know by themselves. Monsters are seen under the bed and in the closet or are the reason the room is a mess. Parents tell their children that they are only imagining things, and hauntings go unreported. Once in a while, a child's involvement with a spirit escalates and mirrors activity in the rest of the house. Only then is the child's encounter understood, even if only through the eyes of a teenager.

For some people, seeing a ghost as a child is a sign of things to come. Many people who report seeing a ghost as an adult say their first experience happened when they were very young. They did not think much of it at the time, but now it all makes sense.

Ellen has a sixth sense. She does not understand it all the time, and she sometimes finds that it gets in the way. But it allows her to see spirits when other people think that everything is normal. She has lived in only two houses, and both were haunted, which leads one to ask whether people with a sixth sense draw the dead to them or if they just see what we do not.

For Ellen, it started when she was only two years old. "I remember seeing a young woman in the back of the apartment, which was an old house divided into four apartments. I would always ask my mom who she was and why she was there. My mom promised me no one was back there, that we were the only two in the house."

Ellen easily convinced herself that she had seen nothing. A child's mind is molded by her parents, and their word is truth. It is unclear whether her mother felt it too, but there was something in the house. She may have been trying to protect her daughter, trying not to scare her. She may have been trying to convince herself. The lie worked. "Soon after, though, I started to not see her, and I didn't have anything happen to me."

She felt an uneasiness over the next few years, but she carefully ignored it. Then, her father and half sister moved in. "My sister and I would hear a little girl laugh every time we were in the end of that house. Then we would both feel someone sit at the ends of our beds when we were trying to sleep at night. It got to the point that we would sleep with my mom in her bed. Of course, this made my mom furious."

The activity slowed down when her father and sister moved out years later. She eventually moved into the room from which she had heard the laughing. "When I got older and finally got brave enough to sleep in the bedroom in the back of the house, it started again. I would hear people talking and see them in the TV. After this, I started begging to move.

My mom, of course, told me no. So I took matters into my own hands. I started getting in fights at school until I got expelled and we had to move."

This was the first time her sixth sense got in the way of her life. They moved into a smaller apartment in Battle Creek, and everything was fine for a while. The quiet did not last long. "About a month after we moved, I was up late because my mom was taking a shower, and I couldn't sleep with the sound of the water in the pipes. I decided to sit up and wait until she was done. All of a sudden, I felt like I was being watched, and a man walked across my room looking straight at me. He was blue with a red shirt and blue shorts. I know that sounds funny, but to a twelve-year-old it was scary. I screamed and ran into the bathroom."

The mysterious blue man raises many questions. While it may have been a twelve-year-old's perspective on something that frightened her, ghosts are usually the color of the people they once were. The blue man, and his casual take on the little girl, point to a possible demon. Those who consider themselves sensitive are more prone to demonic attacks, especially if they embrace their gift.

However scary the man was, Ellen learned to live with her visions. It was usually when someone else got involved that things intensified. "One night, my friend and I were talking, trying to sleep, when we started to get cold, and I felt more uneasy than usual. I saw that man again, only this time it was just his face. We went screaming into the living room and slept there."

As a teenager, Ellen has very little to say about her situation. Her mother cannot move again, and the activity continues. Sometimes the ghosts are different but no less frightening. "I was trying to go to sleep but I couldn't, when all of a sudden I got this terrible feeling of being watched and a feeling of evil. I tried to convince myself that it was nothing until I heard something or someone call my name. I opened my eyes, and a woman was standing there, staring at me. She had on all white and looked evil. I screamed and yelled for my mom, and she came in and comforted me. I haven't been back into my room unless it has been absolutely important."

Ellen sleeps on the floor, wondering why some call her sixth sense a gift.

The Scream on Tape

DENVER, COLORADO

P. T. Barnum rose to fame in the late 1800s and continues to inspire myth and discussion more than a hundred years later. Many feel that he invented the modern circus, and his personality and philosophy play on the imagination as his famed "Greatest Show on Earth" continues across the country, entertaining millions. He was born in Connecticut and set up several homes there, but he found his way to Colorado and built an estate there to winter his circus. Eventually, he become such an influence on the area that it was named after him. Today, there are elementary schools and construction companies there bear his name, but there is also at least one haunted building.

Pink moved to the area when he was eighteen. His house was part of the original P. T. Barnum estate, and the house had all the features of an old and temporary house. It had been built without plumbing, a cellar, or electricity, and the updates to bring modern facilities to the building were only a step above what would be considered adequate.

The move did not feel right from the beginning. "We originally found this house because it was behind my girlfriend's mother's house, which was the heavily renovated servants quarters, complete with coach stable in the rear and huge burns under the carpet, the product of a potbelly stove. My girlfriend had always complained about the house, and was not particularly fond of the fact that we were moving into it." She had told him that there were eyes that stared down at her from the rear window on the second floor.

Pink was not intimidated. He and his friends had experienced the paranormal before and felt that they knew how to handle anything they came across. They also knew, after their first tour of the house, that something was there. "Upon our initial tour of the house, a presence was certainly detectable, but it did not mean harm. In fact, it was somewhat playful. Continuing toward the rear first story of the house, the feeling would become stronger and less playful, but still no malice. Toward the front of the house, things felt playful again. Ascending the stairs, the playful vibe would grow until it would dominate the second floor. That is until you reached the rear bedroom."

He felt different things from the different rooms of the house, but there was something less friendly about that room. "The first time I attempted to enter, I stopped dead in my tracks right inside the doorway. I looked about the small, well-lit, white room and felt the shivers go up my spine."

From the beginning, they knew and accepted that there were ghosts in the house. They lived together, sharing the same physical realm, and the ghosts made themselves known on a consistent basis. "The strongest fingerprint upon that house, other than whatever happened in that rear room, is the presence of a small girl, around the age of twelve. I assume her life was taken by illness, as all of us who had seen her had only seen her in a faded pink nightgown. There was no questioning whether she was around or not. She loved to play."

The other entities would come in and out of their lives, sometimes being seen and other times just being felt. "I worked graveyards with my roommate Syd at a sub shop that closed its doors at 3:00 A.M. We would usually arrive home between 4:00 and 6:00 and would generally relax on the couch and watch a little TV in the living room. Sitting in the living room, watching through our peripheral vision, Syd and I would watch hoards of faint people shuffle about over in the kitchen."

Pink believes he might have caught at least one of the former residents on tape. "I'm a recording artist by hobby. This house was well-suited for home recording, with a central area, dining room, and other such rooms surrounding that would provide isolation. The control was in my bedroom, which was on the second floor in the front of the house." One day, his cat was acting strangely, meowing and moving throughout the house. Alone in the house, Pink decided to record what was going on.

"Upon reviewing the recording, I could hear the cat meowing and the traffic in the background, but something extraordinary was present. There was a very present wobbling type noise that would come and go. This could have been a great number of things, but the factor that ruled out any of those explanations was the fact that the sound was physically moving. Viewing the waveforms, you could see the disruption maintain its frequency, modulation, and decibel levels between tracks. What that means is that this sound was moving around the house, the cat following not far behind. When I mixed that demo, there was a strange sort of scream in the background at the end of a song."

The recording might mean there was something horrific that happened in the house. While they never found out what had happened in the rear bedroom, they did find some evidence of the place's dark history. "Some months after we had moved in, we found a newspaper article from the 1960s about the house. It seems that there was a family living here who had a son with Down syndrome. Long story short, the parents decided to lock the kid in the cellar, where he existed for some years before he was discovered by authorities."

Sometimes a house is filled with negative energy, and sometimes it just draws it in.

Jeff's Song

LONGMONT, COLORADO

Longmont, Colorado, was recently voted one of America's best cities in which to live. It is a place born of the railroads, so it might not be an unusual place for a ghost. When you introduce a talented songwriter into the environment, you never know what the result might be. Although some people are frightened by their ghostly experiences, other people find inspiration in them. Literature is speckled with stories that begin with inexplicable encounters. If ghosts are energy left behind, they may need some kind of trigger to activate them. Music might be the perfect conductor. The mix of electronic equipment and the vibration of strings from a guitar might be the perfect combination to make the sleeper awake.

Jeff brought all of those things to Colorado, but he also had the electric current from his creativity. He was staying with a friend in the Denver suburb in the spring of 2006. It was an old building, known in the town as the Times-Call building because it was the old headquarters of a local newspaper that was printed on the first floor. The upstairs of the building had been closed off since 1964, as evidenced by a calendar hanging on the wall, still open to April 1964. It was filled with old papers and unused bits and pieces when the owner had bought the building.

The neighborhood has a tragic history. In the 1870s, there was an explosion from a gunpowder barrel in the basement of the house next door. It destroyed most of the buildings nearby. "The Dickens Opera House at the end of the street was spared. A bystander, who was standing on top of the opera house at the time of the explosion, was blown off to the roof of a building below. He was spared with an injured leg. A business across the street had all its windows blown in from the shock wave. The woman inside was frantic and ran out of her shop screaming with the blood streaming down from her cuts and bruises," Jeff says.

They soon began rebuilding the block, including printing out of the Times-Call. The owners, who had lived on the second floor, moved out and began to rent out the space. "They rented out rooms, a hot bath, and a meal for people coming and going on the old locomotives and stage coaches. One of the patrons happened to be a semi-famous actress, who must have traveled across the country performing in various venues for the general public. I wish I knew her name."

The years went by, but the building did little to change. The interior was something out of an old Western. "There are old skylights on the ceiling, the wallpaper is slowly peeling off, and the hard wooden floors are warped as if everything is sinking into the middle of the main living room. In fact, the water in the fish tank, against one of the walls, leans toward the center of the room. Watch out for the staircase that leads down to the street level. It leans one side higher than the other, as well, from old age."

Jeff is a longtime musician, who has played in various bands for more than twenty-five years. He has been around the world, including New Zealand and Fiji, and maintains a Web site of his music and appearances (*http://knabel.homestead.com/Homepage.html*). Longmont was just another stop, and he quickly became known in the local music scene. He would write music and play, but once while working on some new music, he saw something out of the corner of his eye.

"I'd been staying there for a few weeks by then, and thought I felt some sort of presence there," he says. He felt it might have been something but kept working until late in the night. He went to bed after putting on a video. Later that night, he felt a cold whisper in his ear.

"I woke up to find the movie still playing and the face of a woman on the TV screen. I felt the hairs on the back of my neck stand up. That was about 2:00 in the morning. I tried to go back to sleep, but my mind was on high alert."

Feeling that something was motivating him, he made some coffee and started to fool around on his guitar. "I felt a presence in the room again, but it felt friendly, as if it liked what I was playing. As I played, I came up with a nice chord progression, some lyrics, and a cool chorus line. An hour or so later, I finished writing my song, called 'U Don't Know.' The vibe in the place was electric."

Jeff shared his experience and his new song with his friend when he came home that morning. He was the owner of the building and had felt something in the place himself, although he had never shared the idea before because he did not want to frighten Jeff. "He said he had had some friends over in the past that felt the same sort of energy that I did. He asked me what the ghost sounded like. I said, 'A woman in her thirties maybe.' He asked me what she looked like. I described her, and his jaw dropped to the floor.

"Joe asked me to wait in the room while he went to get something. He came back ten minutes later with an old photograph he had been keeping in storage with other old artifacts. When he showed me the photo, it was a black-and-white picture of a lady in her late twenties dressed in an old Western theater outfit. She was the same lady I had seen the night before. I was shocked."

The ghost had somehow inspired the song, and she enjoyed the song he had written. "I stayed there for a few more weeks, and every time I played guitar and sang she would let her presence be known. It was a friendly presence as it turned out. So now when I go to visit my friend Joe at the Times-Call building, she lets me know she's still there." The song itself is haunting and can be heard at *www.mp3.com.au/artist.asp?id=28632*.

The Haunted Summerwind Legend

Having a ghost is good for business. Owners of restaurants and hotels know the lure of the paranormal is enough to bring in the curious, and people too intimidated to hit the field with equipment are more than happy to stay at a local haunted bed-and-breakfast. Most haunted businesses are content to let the word out and allow the rumors to bring the money to them. In northern Wisconsin, a local ghost story may have been started to promote a new restaurant. The business venture failed, and all that is left are the stories of the haunted Summerwind Mansion, also known as the Lamont Mansion.

According to a Web site run by the relative of the former owner (*http://summerwindmansion.com*), the property was originally a resort and fishing lodge, and over the next few decades, it underwent massive renovations in an attempt to create a grand residence overlooking West Bay Lake. The owners did not stay long, and the legend is that they were forced out by the ghosts who lay claim to the property. Things went on like that for most of the twentieth century, and with each renovation and each new owner, the myth of the house grew. Misfortune struck each new tenant, like a negative storm coming back every few years to keep the house empty.

Those who have lived there and people in town will tell you the myths are anything but tall tales. There have been unexplained fires, some of which have destroyed parts of the house. A mysterious body was found in one of the crawlspaces and eventually disappeared before it could be reported or confirmed. Not many of the actual hauntings are known, but everyone in the area knows about the mansion's past. The reports come from the old residents who speak of hearing weird noises and of seeing a ghostly woman roam around one of the rooms. Windows were reported to open and close at will, something seen by people from outside the property, as well. It is not much more than an abandoned ruin now, a known haunt investigated by local groups who illegally enter the property.

The stories are keeping the house going, long after it went dark for the last time. Perhaps the property will be opened up again, and whatever lies there will have the chance to touch another family's life.

GLOSSARY

age regression:
The process of going back to a previous time in one's life through the use of hypnosis.

akashic record:
A chart of a person's past lives, future lives, and parallel lives.

apparition:
The visual appearance of any spirit or unusual phenomenon that doesn't necessarily take on the shape of a human form or that doesn't show signs of intelligence or personality.

automatic writing:
A method of communication with the other side that involves using a normal writing instrument and paper.

autonographist:
A professional automatic writer.

channeler:
A person who allows a spirit to temporarily possess his or her body in order for the spirit to be able to communicate with the living.

channeling board:
A tool used for communication with the other side. Also known as a Ouija board or talking board.

clairalience:
The ability to use smell to receive a spirit's message.

clairambience:
The ability to use taste to receive a spirit's message.

clairaudience:
The ability to hear sounds in order to receive a spirit's message.

clairsentience:
The feeling or sensing of a spirit's message.

clairvoyance:
The ability to see the future, or to see objects or events that others can't, using only the eyes and ears.

collective apparition:
An apparition that is seen simultaneously by multiple witnesses.

confabulation:
When real-life experiences are mixed with imagined experiences.

crisis apparition:
A one-time ghostly experience in which the spirit is seen at the time of its death by a loved one.

demon:
One of any nonhuman spirits whose objective is to possess a human.

demonologist:
Someone who studies demons and is well versed in nonhuman activity.

discarnate:
A spirit or ghost.

doppelganger:
The spirit of a person who is living viewed by that same person. A doppelganger often is the vision of one's own death.

ectoplasm:
Residue left behind by ghosts or other paranormal phenomena. Many believe that spirits use ectoplasm to materialize.

electromagnetic field (EMF):
Natural and unnatural fluctuations in the magnetic fields in an area. This field can be measured, and high readings often indicate the presence of a ghost.

electronic voice phenomena (EVP):
The noises and voices that are recorded on traditional audiotape or videotape but aren't audible to the human ear while being recorded—often believed to be voices from the other side.

elemental:
A low-level demon that is closely tied into the elements.

extrasensory perception (ESP):
An awareness of outside happenings or information not attained through the normal human senses.

familiar:
Any animal that is used by a witch for surveillance or for casting spells. A familiar can also be the witch in animal form.

full-bodied apparition:
A ghostly encounter in which a complete human ghost is seen.

ghost:
A visual manifestation of a soul, spirit, life force, or life energy. Most people use this term to describe the visual appearance of a human being or creature that has died and passed on to the other side.

ghost buster:
A person who visits a site that is believed to be haunted with the express purpose of eliminating the ghost or paranormal activity from that location.

ghost hunter:
A person who investigates and studies ghosts, hauntings, and paranormal phenomena.

hypnotherapy:
The treatment of an ailment through the use of hypnosis.

medium:
A person who has a special gift and believes he or she can act as a bridge between the world of the living and the other side.

metaphysics:
A field of study dedicated to the nature of reality.

obsession:
The process by which a demon gains its initial access to a targeted human. The subject literally becomes obsessed with the demon.

orb:
A phenomenon in the shape of a floating ball of light, often thought to be a trapped soul.

other side:
The spirit world, or the place spirits go after death.

paranormal:
Unusual activity that involves ghosts, apparitions, spirits, hauntings, or poltergeists; anything for which there is no scientific explanation.

parapsychology:
The study of phenomena, real or supposed, that appear inexplicable on presently accepted scientific theories.

past-life regression:
The act of using trance or hypnosis to visit former lives.

phenomenon:
A paranormal occurrence that cannot be explained in scientific terms.

physical mediumship:
A form of mediumship in which the spirit communicates using both the physical energies and consciousness of the medium.

place memory:
A location that captures energy and uses it to record an image of an event that once happened there and later replays it.

planchette:
A pointing device used in conjunction with a channeling board.

poltergeist:
A phenomenon that is more often experienced than seen. A poltergeist will often interact with its environment by moving objects, making noises, or making itself known in a variety of other ways.

possession:
The end result of a demonic attack in which a demon takes complete control of its victim.

precursor noise:
A pop or static recorded during an EVP that signals the beginning of a ghostly voice.

progression hypnotherapy:
Visiting future lives through the use of hypnosis.

psi:
Psychic ability or power.

psychic:
A person who uses empathic feelings to tap into non-physical forces.

psychokinesis:
The ability to move objects using only one's mind.

psychosomatics:
A field of study dedicated to the idea that the medical health of a person's body is related to that person's mind and emotions.

reincarnation:
The idea that a soul can be reborn into a new human body.

residual haunting:
A spirit that is trapped in a continuous emotional loop.

sixth sense:
Psychic ability; perception that goes beyond the five senses.

soul loss:
The loss of vital energy experienced as a result of any kind of physical, emotional, mental, or spiritual trauma.

spirit:
An electromagnetic entity in the form of an orb, mist, vortex, or shadow that is the signature of a once-living person who has returned to a specific location.

spirit communicator:
A spirit or ghost that uses a medium in order to communicate with someone either verbally or visually.

spirit operator:
A spirit or ghost that uses a medium to physically manipulate something on earth.

spirit world:
The place spirits go after death.

spiritual guide:
A spirit that watches over a living person and that offers wisdom or guidance.

supernatural:
Anything beyond the accepted definitions of the natural world. Something supernatural is not necessarily ghostly.

superpersonalities:
Negative entities.

table tipping:
One of the original forms of spiritualist ghost communication in which the responses of the spirit are related through movements of a table.

telepathy:
Communication using the mind as opposed to other senses.

time slip:
A displacement in which the witness experiences a different time.

trance mediumship:
A form of mediumship in which the medium shares his or her energy with a spirit through the use of trance.

urban legend:
Any story told as having happened to a friend of a friend. Many reported hauntings are recycled urban legends.

vortex:
A mass of air, water, or energy that spins around very fast, creating a vacuum to pull objects into its empty center.

APPENDIX B

ONLINE RESOURCES

These Web sites are resources created by both professional paranormal investigators as well as amateurs with a sincere interest in the paranormal. You'll find a vast amount of information; so-called "documentation," or evidence, of the paranormal; and case studies. As you explore these and other Web sites, pay attention to the sources of the information and the credibility of each source.

Using any search engine, you can find additional sites relating to the paranormal. Search on keywords such as *ghosts, haunted houses, spirits, poltergeists, paranormal, parapsychology, psychic, hypnotherapy, past-life regression, Ouija board, channeling, mediumship,* or *psychic medium.*

The following Web sites are useful resources for those who want to discover more about various aspects of paranormal activity. Keep in mind that the opinions and theories expressed on these sites are those of the person or people who have created each site and aren't necessarily based on scientific evidence.

General Resources

Adventures Beyond
www.adventuresbeyond.com

Adventures Beyond investigates nearly all facets of the paranormal. From ghosts and hauntings to Bigfoot and UFOs, Adventures Beyond strives to capture evidence of the paranormal on video. Currently, the site offers a documentary series including *Chupacabra*, *America's Most Haunted*, *Witches*, and *Ghosts . . . and Phantoms*. Please check the Web site for ordering information.

Alchemy Lab Web Ring
www.alchemylab.com/webring.htm

This Web site is a Web ring for those interested in gaining further knowledge of alchemy, spiritualism, pagan studies, parapsychology, the paranormal, and many more related topics. Some of the member sites include AstroZone, Spagyria, The Alchemist, Parapsychology, Senshen and the Other World, and Haunted Places.

Alien/UFO/Ghost Research Society
www.alienufoart.com

The Alien/UFO/Ghost Research Society is dedicated to investigating and documenting paranormal activity. The Web site also contains summaries of investigations, ghost stories, and links to additional information.

American Ghost Society
www.prairieghosts.com

The American Ghost Society investigates haunted sites and aids those who believe that they are plagued by the paranormal. Their Web site, Ghosts of the Prairie, provides a mélange of information regarding haunted sites in the United States, ghost hunting, and resources to further your research into the paranormal. This also acts as the main site for author Troy Taylor and offers his books for sale.

American Society for Psychical Research
www.aspr.com

The American Society for Psychical Research is a research organization dedicated to the research and investigation of paranormal activity. The society's Web site is a comprehensive resource for finding additional information on parapsychology topics such as near-death experiences, out-of-body experiences, ESP, psychokinesis, survival after death, and more.

Archive X
www.wirenot.net/X

This Web site serves as an archive of stories and articles relating to the paranormal. It features ghost stories, near-death experiences, stories of angels, out-of-body experiences, and stories and messages of channeling experiences. The Web site also allows you to post your own story or article if you have an experience to share.

Committee for Skeptical Inquiry

www.csicop.org

The Committee for Skeptical Inquiry is a committee designed to investigate claims of paranormal activity from a scientific standpoint. Its Web site offers a variety of resources for those interested in researching the validity of paranormal experiences. Articles cover topics such as poltergeist activity, clairvoyance, reincarnation, psychics, and hauntings.

Earthbound Ghosts

www.erols.com/rcod

Earthbound is a Web site that offers not only proof of life after death but also previews of documented conversations with ghosts. Through the use of a channeler, ghosts are able to tell their tale. Most of the time, they don't realize that they are dead. The Web site also offers links to additional resources.

Ghost Chat

www.psychics.co.uk/ghostchat.html

This Web site opens the doors of communication for those who would like to chat with people expressing the same interest in the paranormal. Share stories, ask questions, play games, find downloads—this Web site is a one-stop shop for your paranormal needs.

Ghost Hunters Inc.
www.angelfire.com/tx3/ghosthtml
Ghost Hunters Inc. is interested in the research of paranormal activity. The group conducts investigations and strives to discover scientific proof of the paranormal. Their Web site offers summaries of investigations; ghost hunting tips, stories and photographs; and links to additional information.

The Ghost Hunter's Society
http://members.tripod.com/GhostHuntersSociety/Home.htm
The Ghost Hunter's Society conducts private investigations and documents paranormal activity. Its Web site offers a frequently-asked-questions page, true ghost stories and experiences, summaries of investigations, a photograph collection, information for joining the society, and links to additional information.

Ghost Research Society
www.ghostresearch.org
The Ghost Research Society is dedicated to the research and documentation of paranormal activity and conducts private investigations. Its Web site offers articles related to the paranormal, photographs, a listing and history of haunted sites, and links to additional information.

Ghosts and Other Haunts

www.go.to/nzghosts

This Web site offers a collection of photographs of the paranormal and brief descriptions of the circumstances surrounding these pictures. You also will find a collection of ghost stories from both New Zealand and Ireland, as well as several links to additional information.

Ghost Shop

www.ghostshop.com

This Web site is an interesting source of information for those curious about electronic voice phenomena. Here you will find guidelines for creating your own microphone for use in picking up EVP, an opportunity to listen to recordings of EVP, facts about this phenomenon, and links for more resources to further your study.

Ghostvillage.com

www.ghostvillage.com

This is by far the best and the most complete site on the Internet for people interested in the paranormal. It has a message board with almost a quarter of a million postings, accounts from witnesses, paranormal news, and classes. It is also the main site for Jeff Belanger, one of the leading authors in the paranormal field, and you can purchase his books directly from the site.

Haunted Places Directory
www.haunted-places.com

This Web site is exactly what it sounds like—a directory of haunted sites around the world. Here, you will find not only listings of haunted sites but also links to other organizations dedicated to the research of paranormal activity, a collection of true ghost stories, a bookstore, and media coverage of the paranormal.

International Ghost Hunters Society
www.ghostweb.com

The International Ghost Hunters Society comprises several groups and individuals dedicated to the investigation and documentation of paranormal activity. Its Web site offers a wealth of information regarding the paranormal. Included are photographs, videos, articles, stories, EVPs, a home-study course, support-group information, a recommended-reading list, membership information, and links to additional information.

The L.I.F.E. Foundation
www.paranormalhelp.com

The L.I.F.E. (Living in Fear Ends) Foundation is dedicated to helping those who are plagued by the paranormal. This foundation serves as a support group for people in need. The Web site offers articles, media information, procedures for getting help, advice, and links to additional information and help. This site also documents one of the most traumatic and engaging cases in American history.

New England Society for Psychic Research
www.warrens.net

The New England Society for Psychic Research is dedicated to researching and investigating paranormal activities. Its Web site offers summaries of investigations, photographs of the paranormal, and links to additional information. The society also offers membership. This site can be used as a reference for investigations in Connecticut and in other states.

Obiwan's UFO-Free Paranormal Page
www.ghosts.org

This Web site offers answers to frequently asked questions concerning ghosts, stories and photographs of the paranormal, a listing of haunted sites, guidelines for ghost-story submissions, and links to additional information. This is one of the oldest and remains one of the best paranormal Web sites.

The Paranormal Network
www.mindreader.com

This is the Web site of famous paranormal investigator Loyd Auerbach. Here you will find a biography of Auerbach in relation to his work with the paranormal, general information about the Office of Paranormal Investigations, and links to additional information.

The Shadowlands
http://theshadowlands.net

This is one of the most extensive resources for haunted locations around the world. If you see a list of places on a regional site, it most likely came from The Shadowlands. Not all of the information is accurate, but it is the closest thing right now to a database of the paranormal. The site also has information on ghosts and a message board.

An Unknown Encounter
www.barcon.com

This Web site allows the viewer to preview clips of paranormal activity caught on video. If you like what you see, you can order the full-length video online. This site also features video equipment for rent and camera crews for hire. If you are interested in video-recording paranormal activity, check out this Web site for further information.

Paranormal Media: Magazines, Television, and Radio Shows

Beyond Reality Radio
http://beyondrealityradio.com

This is the radio show hosted by the members of The Atlantic Paranormal Society. The show is a land-based one, but you can listen live on the Internet and download archived shows.

BlogTalkRadio

www.blogtalkradio.com

This is the main page for BlogTalkRadio. Once on the site, you can search for paranormal radio shows by topic. Some of the better shows on the site are from Annette and the Crossroads Paranormal Radio Crew.

Coast to Coast AM/Dreamland

www.coasttocoastam.com

This is the main site for the *Coast to Coast* and *Dreamland* radio shows. *Coast to Coast* is the oldest and most respected paranormal radio show. The content of the page is worth the visit, although both shows are primarily terrestrial. Both the shows and the archives can be accessed for a fee.

FATE

www.fatemag.com

FATE (an acronym for Fantastic Adventures and True Experiences) is a monthly publication featuring true accounts of paranormal activity. The magazine's Web site offers the current issue's articles, as well as guidelines for submissions.

The Ghost Chronicles

www.toginet.com

The Ghost Chronicles is a live show offered through this site (click on Talk Shows), but you also can listen to replays of the show (check the schedule). The show is worth a listen, and there are plans to archive

it. Another variation of the show can be heard at *www
.ghostvillage.com*.

Ghost!

http://ghostmag.com

Ghost! is one of the most respected of the new paranormal magazines. The site has information on the
publication but not much more in the way of content.

Haunted Times

www.hauntedtimes.com

This is the main site for *Haunted Times* magazine,
and it offers a message board and information on the
publication. The site also has online articles.

Mysteries Magazine

http://mysteriesmagazine.com

Mysteries is probably the best of the new paranormal magazines and offers information on ghosts and
other elements of the unknown. The site offers reviews
of books and movies as well as evidence sent in by
readers.

Spooky Southcoast

www.spookysouthcoast.com

This site is for the radio show *Spooky Southcoast*.
Although its primary focus is the southeastern section
of Massachusetts, the show often has subjects of more
universal appeal. It has covered topics such as demons,
hauntings, and issues in paranormal investigating.

Unsolved Mysteries

www.unsolvedmysteries.com

This Web site is for anyone who has a story to tell about paranormal activity. It allows you to post your story and ask questions about ghosts, UFOs, ESP, or any other mystery that interests you. Your story will be added to the archive, and others will have an opportunity to respond to it. Or, if you don't have a story of your own, you can feel free to browse the stories of others and respond to their inquiries if you choose. This Web site is not affiliated with the television show.

The 'X' Zone Radio Show

www.xzone-radio.com

The 'X' Zone is hosted by Rob McConnell and is on the air nightly for four hours. It offers many supernatural topics and often has live psychic readings.

PARANORMAL GROUPS AND INVESTIGATORS BY STATE

This section features some of the paranormal groups and investigators in different states. This list is far from exhaustive, and a simple Internet search will provide more detail. Some of the information here is about specific, well-known cases in the state. Some of these groups offer help with the paranormal, while some only document their work. Many are located in one state but investigate and offer information on other locations.

Alabama

Northern Alabama Paranormal Research Society
www.naprs.us

Alabama Ghost Hunter's Society
http://ghostinvestigator.tripod.com/ghostinvestigators

Alaska

Investigation of Paranormal in Alaska
www.freewebs.com/iopialaska

Arizona

Ghost 2 Ghosts Arizona
www.arizona.ghost2ghosts.co.uk

Arkansas

Arkansas Paranormal Investigations
http://paranormalbeliever.com

Central Arkansas Society for Paranormal Research
www.casprquest.com

California

American Paranormal Investigations
www.ap-investigations.com

Bay Area Paranormal Investigations
www.bayareaparanormal.com

Colorado

CCPI
www.candcparanormal.com

Rocky Mountain Paranormal Research Society
www.rockymountainparanormal.com

Connecticut
Connecticut Paranormal Research Society
www.cprs.info

Northwest Connecticut Paranormal Society
http://northwestconnecticutparanormal.com

Delaware
Delaware Ghost Hunters
www.delawareghosthunters.com

M-and-M-Investigators
www.m-and-m-investigators.com

Florida
Daytona Beach Paranormal Research Group, Inc
www.dbprginc.org

Infinity Para-Investigations Network
www.infinityparanormal.com

Georgia
Georgia Haunt Hunt Team
www.geocities.com/gahaunt

Hawaii
Kwaidan
www.geocities.com/Area51/Hollow/6166

Idaho
Idaho Spirit Seekers
www.idahospiritseekers.com

Illinois
Haunted Chicago
www.hauntedchicago.com

TRIPAR Research Organization
www.triparinvestigations.org

Indiana
Crossroads Paranormal
www.crossroadsparanormal.com

Proof Paranormal
http://proofparanormal.com/index2.html

Iowa
Iowa Center for Paranormal Research
www.iowacenterforparanormalresearch.com

Kansas
Miller's Paranormal Research
www.millersparanormalresearch.com

Kentucky
Kentucky Paranormal Research
www.kyghosts.com

TM Ghost Hunters
http://tmghosthunters.com

Louisiana
Ghosts in Louisiana
www.hollowhill.com/la/louisiana-ghosts.htm

Maine
Maine Supernatural
http://mysite.verizon.net/vzeqnk8x

Maryland
Maryland Paranormal Investigators
www.angelfire.com/md/MPInvestigators

Massachusetts
Berkshire Paranormal Group
www.berkshireparanormal.com

Massachusetts Paranormal Crossroads
www.masscrossroads.com

New England Ghost Project
www.neghostproject.com

Michigan
Faces from the Grave
www.facesfromthegrave.mirrorz.com

West Michigan Ghost Hunters Society
www.wmghs.com

Minnesota
MinnesotaGhosts.com
www.minnesotaghosts.com

Minnesota Paranormal Investigators Group
http://minnesotaparanormalinvestigators.com

Mississippi
Haunted Mississippi
www.prairieghosts.com/hauntms.html

Missouri
Missouri Ghost Hunters Societies
http://ghosthaunting.com

Montana
Montana Paranormal Research Society
www.mtprs.org

Nebraska
Haunted Nebraska
www.prairieghosts.com/hauntne.html

Nevada
Nevada Spooks
www.nvspooks.com

New Hampshire
ECTOWEB
www.ectoweb.com

New Jersey
New Jersey Ghost Hunters Society
www.njghs.net

New Journey Ghost Research
www.njghostresearch.org

New Mexico
New Mexico Paranormal Investigations
www.nmparanormal.com

New York
Long Island Paranormal Investigators
www.liparanormalinvestigators.com

New York Paranormal
www.newyorkparanormal.i8.com

New York Pennsylvania Paranormal Society
www.freewebs.com/xxghostsandspiritsxx

North Carolina
Coalition of Autonomous Scientific
Paranormal Entity Researchers
www.geocities.com/casper_research/Main_page

Eastern Paranormal
www.easternparanormal.com

North Dakota
North Dakota Ghosthunters and Paranormal Investigators
http://ghostinvestigator.tripod.com/ndgis

Ohio
Ghost Hunters Ohio Search Team
www.ohioghosthunter.com

Ghosts of Ohio
www.ghostsofohio.org

Oklahoma
Ghost Haunts of Oklahoma and Urban
Legend Investigations
www.ghouli.org

Oregon
Salem Spirit Trackers
http://home.comcast.net/~noticky/wsb/html/view
.cgi-home.html-.html

Pennsylvania
Ghosts of Gettysburg
www.ghostsofgettysburg.com

Pennsylvania Ghost Hunters Society
http://roswell.fortunecity.com/goldendawn/76/index.html

Rhode Island
Haunted! Paranormal Research Society
www.hauntedprs.org

New England Anomalies Research & Investigations
http://nearparanormal.com

South Carolina
Carolina Paranormal Research
http://carolinaparanormal.net

Tennessee
The Bell Witch
www.bellwitch.org

Tennessee Ghost Hunters
www.tnghosthunters.com

Texas
Lone Star Spirits
www.lonestarspirits.org

Society for Psychical Research
www.spr.ac.uk/expcms/index.php?section=1

Utah
Paranormal Investigations Team of Utah
www.piteamofutah.com

Vermont
Vermont Agency of Paranormal Organized Research
www.teamvapor.org

Virginia
Hampton Roads Paranormal Research Group
www.geocities.com/Area51/8497

Washington, DC Metro Area Ghost Watchers
www.dchauntings.com

Washington
Advanced Ghost Hunters of Seattle-Tacoma
www.aghost.us

Washington State Paranormal Investigations
and Research
www.wspir.com

West Virginia
West Virginia Ghost Hunters
www.westvirginiaghosthunters.com

Wisconsin
Wausau Paranormal Research Society
www.pat-wausau.org

Wyoming
Wyoming Paranormal Investigators
http://wyparanormalinvestigators.com

INDEX

Index

Index